Handbook
for
Writing
Proposals

Handbook for Writing Proposals

Robert J. Hamper
L. Sue Baugh

NTC Business Books
NTC/Contemporary Publishing Group

Library of Congress Cataloging-in-Publication Data

Hamper, Robert J.
    Handbook for writing proposals / Robert J. Hamper, L. Sue Baugh.
       p.   cm.
    Includes bibliographical references and index.
    ISBN 0-8442-3273-4 (cloth)
    ISBN 0-8442-3274-2 (paper)
    1. Proposal writing in business.   2. Proposal writing in research.
I. Baugh, L. Sue.   II. Title.
HF5718.5.H2844   1995
658.15'224—dc20   94-17748
                        658.15   CIP
                        HAM

Published by NTC Business Books
A division of NTC/Contemporary Publishing Group, Inc.
4255 West Touhy Avenue, Lincolnwood (Chicago), Illinois 60646-1975 U.S.A.
Copyright © 1995 by NTC/Contemporary Publishing Group, Inc.
Printed in the United States of America
International Standard Book Number: 0-8442-3273-4 (cloth)
                                      0-8442-3274-2 (paper)

20   19   18   17   16   15   14   13   12   11   10   9   8   7   6   5   4

≡Contents

$\equiv$ DEDICATION

To Our Parents

$\equiv$ PREFACE

In the 1990s, a record number of people are going into business for themselves, either on their own or with others. To survive, they must learn quickly how to attract and win clients.

If you have launched your business, are thinking about doing so, or simply want to improve your proposal process—*Handbook for Writing Proposals* is for you. In this book, you will discover how to find bids, how to evaluate which bids you have the best chance of winning, and how to develop winning proposals, including personal client presentations.

HOW TO USE THIS BOOK

You can work straight through this book—from Chapter 1 to Chapter 8—or find the chapter that provides the specific information you need. We cover eight essential topics:

1. *How do you know where to start?* Chapter 1 explains that the real starting point is developing your marketing strategy. What business are you in and why are you in it? By knowing your business strategy, you will be able to target customers and bids that support your strategy and increase your chances of building a successful business.

2. *What is the proposal process?* Chapter 2 provides an overview of the 9-step proposal process. This chapter briefly describes the steps you need to take from the moment the RFP arrives through the final proposal production and client presentation stages.

3. *How do you select a project and choose a proposal team?* Chapters 1 and 3 give you general guidelines for making a bid/ no-bid decision to avoid going after too many bids or pursuing bids you have little chance of winning. Chapter 3 also shows

you how to build an effective proposal team. The final section in this chapter describes how to find market research information easily and quickly by setting up computer searches. We provide a list of major databases available to any firm.

4. *What is your unique selling point?* What do you have to offer the client that will make you stand out from your competition? Chapter 4 discusses ways to find the client's stated and unstated needs that can inspire your unique selling point.

5. *How do you create the best program design?* Clients want to know what you can do for them and why you, in particular, should be hired. Chapter 5 explains in detail how you can develop a solid, powerful program design that shows potential clients that you understand their needs, have the best solution to their problems, and are the best company for the job.

6. *What goes into a complete proposal?* The body of the proposal is only part of what makes up a winning document. Chapter 6 shows you how to develop an effective cover letter and an executive summary and how to establish a format for your proposal design. Clients must be able to find their way through your proposal easily.

7. *How do you use graphics and illustrations?* With today's graphics software and laser printers, even small companies can produce impressive documents. Chapter 7 focuses on producing your proposal, particularly the effective use of graphics and illustrations.

8. *How do you make an effective client presentation?* Translating your written proposal into a winning presentation is as much art as science. Chapter 8 covers the process from initial planning, organization, and practice to the actual presentation itself— setting up for success and handling troublesome questions from the client.

SPECIAL FEATURES OF THIS BOOK

Whether you are new at writing proposals or an experienced hand, you will find these features helpful.

- **Forms and checklists.** Each chapter offers sample forms, checklists, and questions to stimulate your thinking and help you develop forms tailored to your particular company.

- **Samples of proposal formats.** Throughout this book, you will find samples of refusal letters, cover letters, proposal tables of contents and title pages, executive summaries, resume boilerplates, and proposals themselves.

- **Samples of graphics and illustrations.** Chapter 7 provides clear examples of how and why different types of graphics are used and when to use them.

- **Summaries of key points.** Throughout the book we summarize the key points discussed to give you a quick reference list.

PLAN, PREPARE, PRACTICE

The business climate today is full of risk and opportunity. You need every competitive edge possible. *Handbook for Writing Proposals* was designed to help you plan, prepare, and practice to create a successful business. We hope this book helps you minimize your risks and make the most of your opportunities. We wish you the best.

Robert J. Hamper
River Forest, Illinois

L. Sue Baugh
Evanston, Illinois

CHAPTER
≡ONE

WHERE TO BEGIN?

Tracy Masters, a consultant at Andover Medical Consultants, set the newspaper in front of her colleague, Ed Breen, and pointed to a headline in the business pages: "BioCom Seeks Proposals for New Drug Treatment Software."

"Our company is going after this job," she said. "BioCom wants software developed that will give them a uniform medical format for handling drug treatment data from centers all over the country. Ms. Reiner has asked us to be part of the proposal development team."

"That's great!" Breen said. "But we've never written proposals before."

"So we'll learn how—it can't be that hard. We've got experience in handling drug treatment data and in developing medical format software. Just get ready for some long hours."

        •   •   •

Alan Hildago's small healthcare public relations firm had been hit hard by a downturn in the economy. Searching for new ideas, he noticed a significant gap in patient education materials in most medical association publication catalogs. Here was a niche his company could fill. He explained his idea to his writing staff.

"Our proposal has to convince corporate sponsors and medical associations that putting money into fancy advertisements isn't nearly as effective as spending dollars on patient education and communication materials we can develop. Let's make a proposal to three of our pharmaceutical clients and the pediatric association we worked for last year. They know our work, and they're likely to listen to us."

        •   •   •

Lynn Wong-Brink spread the requests for proposals across her desk. Her information services company was new in the marketplace, so it seemed to make sense to try for any and all jobs her firm had even a remote chance of winning. Fanned out in front of her was a government contract for upgrading educational databases, a municipal study to examine the feasibility of installing mobile phones in city trucks, and a corporate contract to develop monthly overseas economic analyses and forecasts.

Admittedly, her staff would be stretched a little thin on the government or corporate job, but they could do the work with a little luck and extra hours. She put her staff to work on the three proposals.

"What if we get more than one of these jobs?" her financial analyst asked.

"We'll worry about that when the time comes," she said.

These three scenarios illustrate some of the most common opportunities and pitfalls of proposal writing. In the first scenario, the firm has targeted the right market, but the proposal-writing team is less than knowledgeable about how to respond to the request. If the team doesn't learn in time, the company will lose out in the bidding war.

The second scenario represents a good match of company skills and client needs. In addition, the firm's consultants know the client, and the client is familiar with the firm's work. The company can emphasize its strengths based on the consultants' past association with the client. Because this is an unsolicited proposal, the task facing the proposal-writing team is to persuade the client that the firm's ideas should replace the client's current policy. If the team does its homework well, this firm has a good chance of getting its proposal accepted.

The third scenario describes one of the most tempting pitfalls that companies encounter: the temptation to shoot at every target and hope you hit at least one. Lynn has made little effort to match client needs to her company's services and skills. Even if a proposal is accepted, Lynn has no way to assure the client that her firm can do the job within the proposed time and cost constraints. If more than one proposal is accepted, there may not be enough staff to do any job well. At the very least, the company will waste a lot of time, money, and effort writing proposals for jobs it has little chance of winning or completing to the client's satisfaction.

TYPES OF PROPOSALS

A proposal is primarily a sophisticated sales piece that seeks to define a client's problem and/or opportunities and to sell the client on your company's ability to provide solutions and strategies. To begin, it may be helpful to distinguish the types of proposals you or your company may write. Proposals generally fall into one of the following four categories.

Internal Proposals

Internal proposals are written within a company by a particular division, department, group, or individual to persuade top management to support an idea or project. For example, the product line manager may write a proposal to automate a particular assembly process. Even though they are for internal consumption only, these proposals follow the same principles as proposals written for outside companies or agencies.

Solicited Proposals

Sometimes, a company is formally invited to submit a proposal—they receive a request for proposal (RFP), request for quotation (RFQ), or bid invitation. The client has a particular project or problem and is looking for outside help to get the job done. The RFP or bid invitation outlines the requirements and criteria for the job, and the client selects a supplier on the basis of a firm's recommended program, qualifications, and projected costs.

Unsolicited Proposals

These proposals are the most risky to write because they may require considerable time and effort to develop, with no guarantee that a client will be interested in the product or service offered. For example, a firm may develop a program or concept, such as a new accounting method, and then must persuade clients to contract for the service. Because the client has not requested the proposal, the firm must compete with a client's internal operations and other businesses for the client's attention and acceptance.

On the other hand, these proposals do represent a way to generate new business for a company. As a rule, however, companies do not write unsolicited proposals unless they have considerable marketing evidence that such proposals are likely to succeed.

Sole-Source Contracts

In some instances, a government agency or private firm or association will contract with only one company to supply a product or service, generally when the company has established an outstanding record of reliability and performance. A proposal for a sole-source contract is done not to compete for a job but simply to comply with regulations. The format is often standardized and requests detailed information about the product, delivery schedules, and pricing. Your marketing research should be able to tell you when a supposedly open contract RFP is actually "wired," or targeted, for a specific company. This means your firm has only a remote chance of winning the contract and you should consider not submitting a proposal.

Exhibit 1.1 summarizes these four types of proposals and their characteristics.

Exhibit 1.1   Proposals and Their Characteristics

Internal proposal

Written within a company by a particular division, department, group, or individual in the firm; it may be solicited or
unsolicited.

Advantages—Those preparing the proposal know the
firm's needs and the management structure; communication
may be easier and decisions made more quickly than with
outside clients.

Disadvantages—The proposal must compete with other
company business for scarce resources; if the proposal loses
its management champion, the project may be canceled.

Solicited proposal

Written in response to an RFP from a potential client.

Advantages—Client is requesting a proposal, and the
firm can select which RFPs to answer based on resources,
expertise, previous experience, and time/cost calculations.

Disadvantages—If the firm's bid/no bid decision-making
process is flawed, firm may use up valuable resources
researching, writing, and presenting the proposal with little
chance of obtaining the project.

Unsolicited proposal

Proposals that a company initiates without an RFP and sends
to potential clients in an effort to obtain new business.

Advantages—The firm can introduce itself to a wide
range of companies; the same proposal can be sent to many
firms, thus conserving company resources.

Disadvantages—Proposals are not tailored to individual
companies; the firm may get more business than it can
successfully handle.

Sole-source contracts

Primarily government projects that are tied into a specific
firm; the RFP does not request a competitive bid but, to
satisfy regulations, elicits detailed information on the product
or services to be supplied.

Advantages—The firm contracted to do the work knows
when the work will be coming in and the specifications; no
resources are required to win the contract.

(Continued)

> *Disadvantages*—If another firm responds to the RFP, it has little or no chance of winning the contract away from the company currently doing the work. If the contract *is* awarded to the bidding firm, they may have to use the specifications and parameters of the prior contractor.

THREE KEY QUESTIONS: CREATING YOUR BUSINESS PLAN, DEVELOPING YOUR MARKETING STRATEGY, AND LOCATING NEW BUSINESS*

When it comes to developing winning proposals, it doesn't matter whether your company is a Fortune 500 firm or a new venture on the block. The basic questions you need to answer are the same:

- How do you get requests for proposals (RFPs) or locate job opportunities?
- How do you choose which jobs your firm should target?
- How do you write a winning proposal?

It may come as a surprise that the key to eliciting RFPs or RFQs, or to locating job opportunities is not to hire a professional proposal writer but first *to develop an effective business plan and marketing strategy.* A business plan defines who the company is, what it does, how it should position itself in the marketplace to capture the largest market share possible, how it can best adapt to change, and how it will earn a reasonable profit. It includes a mission statement that spells out in a brief statement what business the company is in and what its main objectives are in terms of product or service line and return on investment.

The marketing strategy should support the objectives of the business plan and help the company achieve its goals and increase it profitability. For example, if a computer manufacturer suddenly finds its current target consumers switching from personal computers (PCs) to laptop

---

* For more detailed information on establishing a business plan and marketing strategy, see Hamper and Baugh, *Strategic Market Planning,* Lincolnwood, IL: NTC Business Books, 1990.

computers, a marketing strategy can help the company reposition itself either to switch to the laptop product line or to find new markets for its PCs.

A marketing strategy can help you zero in on a target market, or niche, that emphasizes your strengths and minimizes your weaknesses. In effect, you narrow the field of potential clients to those you can serve exceptionally well, thus cultivating a reputation as a problem-solving firm. This approach can increase your chances of success for any proposal you write.

With a marketing strategy, your emphasis changes from simply selling products or services to selling *service* to clients, a subtle but powerful shift in philosophy. This requires that you research your clients to discover what needs or problems they have that *you are uniquely qualified to help them solve,* those jobs that no one else can do as well as you. The approach changes from "Here are the services and skills we provide" to "Here is how our services and skills can help to solve *your* problems and assist *your* growth."

Finally, a marketing strategy helps you take a longer view of business cycles and enables you to develop contingency plans for anticipating and responding to change. In the 1990s and beyond, national and international competition both within an industry and between industries is going to get a lot tougher. Everything from political systems to workplace technology to personal skills is undergoing rapid, unprecedented change. To survive, companies must use their marketing strategy to spot the opportunities that change brings and to adapt quickly, imaginatively, and effectively to new circumstances.

In summary, a business plan and marketing strategy enable you to:

- Identify your company's goals and objectives.
- Define your company's main strengths and weaknesses.
- Identify market niches in which your firm has an advantage over the competition.
- Identify potential clients within those niches and how you can help solve those clients' problems.
- Establish contingency plans to anticipate and adapt to a rapidly changing marketplace.

In today's environment, a well-defined marketing strategy can serve as a blueprint to guide your firm as it seeks new business opportunities.

It is well worth your time to learn how to devise such a strategy for your firm, whether you are a one-person sole proprietorship or part of a multinational corporate team.

LOCATING NEW BUSINESS

Once your firm has a clear understanding of its target market, the next step is obtaining business—whether from previous clients or new clients. Firms have several sources of business leads, including government and private agencies/nonprofit groups, industry, and informal networks.

One word of caution: Because funding practices and policies change so rapidly in today's environment, specific names and addresses for sources become outdated almost as quickly as they are published. Your best approach is to visit the reference section of your local public library and government printing office to obtain the latest information on federal, state, city, and private/nonprofit agency contracts and grants.

Government and Private Agencies/Nonprofit Groups

Government agencies from the federal level to local city councils contract with outside suppliers for many services. The *Commerce Business Daily,* published by the U.S. Department of Commerce, provides information on federal procurement invitations, contract awards, and subcontracting leads. An electronic edition that can be accessed by computer is also available.

Some major cities also have private or government grant centers that provide a wide range of information on municipal, corporate, and private/nonprofit agency grants and contracts. The Donors' Forum in Chicago, Illinois, is a good example of this type of resource. The U.S. Small Business Administration also has roughly four hundred small business development centers across the country. Many universities cooperate with state and federal governments to create "small business incubators," resource groups that specialize in helping small businesses acquire information, technical resources, and funds. Again, your local reference librarian can help you locate the names and addresses of these centers. Many of their services are free to the public.

Industry Sources

Industry publications, associations, and funding centers list RFPs, contracts, and grants open for bidding. Such information is usually free to the public or can be obtained for a nominal fee or subscription rate.

Networks

The sources listed above represent the formal method of finding new business. Networks—your personal contacts with individuals working in industry, government, and private offices and agencies—represent informal and often far more effective sources of new business leads.

Networks can be built through contacts with people in industry associations; through client contacts and referrals; through volunteer work you do for various industry, government, and nonprofit agencies; and through personal friendships and professional relationships. People in your network will often supply essential background information on contracts and grants that can make the difference between winning or losing a job.

Your network contacts can keep you abreast of new contracts or grants coming up that may be suited to your firm. This advance warning can give you a jump on the competition. By the time the RFP or grant guidelines are published, you will be well into your research and writing phases of the proposal process.

Having the inside story on contracts and grants can be an invaluable asset for your firm. Make sure that you give top priority to cultivating and maintaining your networks, particularly in today's environment, where more firms are going after fewer dollars.

WHICH JOBS TO TARGET

Although it may seem like a good strategy to go after all the job prospects that you have even a remote chance of winning, actually the reverse is true. The more accurately you target specific projects that match your firm's capabilities, the more successful you are likely to be. It is important to satisfy your clients' needs as thoroughly as possible, because your business depends on good referrals and recommendations from previous clients. Again, this is where a sound marketing strategy can keep you focused on your market niche and prevent you from going in too many directions or chasing jobs that are only remotely related to your principle line of business.

But how do you decide which jobs your firm will pursue? This important preliminary process starts with top management, whether a corporate hierarchy or one person who owns the entire business.

Management Responsibility

One of your first steps will be to develop a decision-making process that goes into action the moment an RFP or new business opportunity arrives. This process can be part of your firm's standard operating procedure for proposal writing. Key elements of the process should include the following:

- As soon as an RFP or other bid opportunity comes into the office, it must be reported to the person responsible for that area. The individual may be a vice president, contracts officer, or program manager. This policy ensures that no one sits on an RFP or contract bid and loses valuable time.

- Management should call a bid-decision meeting to assess whether a proposal should be written. If management decides that the company has a realistic chance of winning the job, a proposal should be prepared.

- Proposals should be assigned to those staff members most qualified to address the clients' concerns. Managers must ensure that these staff members have enough time to do the job well, and are not forced to develop the proposal on the side.

- If a team is assembled to write the proposal, it should have a specified area in which to work, free from distractions or interruptions.

Bid-Decision Criteria

At the bid-decision meeting, assess each RFP or new opportunity in light of the following criteria:

1. *First and most important, does the proposal support your total marketing strategy?* The bids you decide to pursue should be in line with your mission statement and primary marketing goals. For example, if the goal of your firm is to increase business in city traffic planning contracts, an RFP from a healthcare firm will pull you off your main objective. Make sure the jobs you pursue support your business plan and marketing strategy.

2. *Does this project fall into your organization's area of expertise?* For example, if the RFP deals with upgrading satellite communications relays and you are only beginning to venture into that area, do you have sufficient skills and resources to handle the job? Nothing kills a company's reputation faster than failure to perform the required work. Make sure you have the capability to follow through on the job. Otherwise, it's best to decline an RFP rather than risk compromising your firm's reputation.

3. *Does your background research on the project point out where your firm has a competitive edge over other companies?* Do you have more experience in this area? Is your staff better trained or educated? Can you come up with more innovative solutions to the clients' problems? If you cannot find some competitive edge, it may be better to wait for the next opportunity.

4. *Have you worked for the client before or had significant contact with them on other jobs?* If so, you often have a unique vantage point regarding their operations and problems. This fact can help give you a competitive edge over other firms.

5. *Can you assemble a proposal team and provide them with enough support and dedicated time to get the job done?* If your team does not have enough time or management support to write the best proposal, you decrease your chances of winning the contract.

6. *Finally, taking all other criteria into consideration, what are the realistic chances that your firm will receive the contract?* If your research shows you have any less than a 50 to 60 percent chance of winning a job, it is generally not worth your time to pursue it. Some experts say that a firm should not pursue any job unless they have an 80 percent or better chance of winning the contract.

Also, see if you can determine whether another firm has been unofficially selected, or "wired," to get the contract or job. Your personal network contacts should be able to give you this information.

When *Not* to Write a Proposal

If any one or more of the following criteria hold true, you should seriously consider declining the RFP or job opportunity. Chances are the solicitation has been made simply to satisfy regulations or to comply with federal or state laws.

- The timeframe for preparing and submitting a proposal is completely unrealistic for you to do a good job.
- The RFP states that the current project is follow-up work for a multiple-stage project; you would be competing against a firm that has completed the first part of the project. (However, you may be able to subcontract with the original firm to do a portion of the work.)
- The technical or other specifications of the project do not match your systems but do match those of your competitors.
- The contract does not support your marketing strategy or is out of your field of expertise.
- You have no real competitive edge over other firms.
- You do not have the staff or resources to prepare the best proposal your company can present.
- Your chances of winning the proposal are less than 50 percent or, as some experts advocate, less than 80 percent.

CHARACTERISTICS OF A WINNING PROPOSAL

If the RFP or new opportunity meets the bid-decision criteria, your task now shifts from deciding "Should we do this proposal?" to "How do we write a winning proposal?" Whether you are responding to an RFP or initiating the proposal, remember that your overriding purpose is to convince the client that *your firm is uniquely qualified to do the job.*

From the client's perspective, proposals make it possible to evaluate the skills and capabilities of a select range of companies and to choose the best firm for the job.

No matter who the prospective client may be and what problems must be solved, a winning proposal will always include at least the following elements:

1. *Evidence that you clearly understand the client's problem or situation.* It is astonishing how many proposals show little indication that the submitting firm has taken the time to research the client's problem and to state it clearly. This element is so important that it should be placed first in the proposal format.

2. *A strategy and program plan or design that the client feels will solve the problem and produce the desired results.* The strategy and program plan are the heart of the proposal. They describe how you are going to solve the client's problems, and they must be carefully tailored to each client's needs. The proposal must tell the client enough without telling them everything. Otherwise, they may use your proposal to do the job themselves!

3. *Clear documentation of your firm's qualifications and capabilities for carrying out the program plan.* The client must be convinced that your firm has the required expertise and staff to accomplish the work better than anyone else. This documentation can take the form of a list of previous client work and resumes of staff members.

4. *Evidence that your firm is reliable and dependable.* You may want to give reference or client contacts who will vouch for your firm. The new client must have confidence that you will deliver on your promises and will complete the job within the time and cost estimates you have developed.

5. *A convincing reason why the client should choose your firm over all the others competing for the job.* Do you have a better program plan, more expertise in the field, better staff, or some other competitive edge? Highlight this advantage; clients should feel they can't afford to do without you.

6. *Finally, your proposal should **look** like a winner.* The format, graphics, printing, and binding should convey the spirit and professionalism of your company. With the desktop publishing

programs available to even one-person operations, there is no reason why you cannot turn out proposals that display your company's ideas and qualifications in the best light.

In the chapters that follow, you will learn how to develop a winning proposal, step by step—from the initial analysis of a client's situation, to development of a program strategy, to production of the final written proposal. Once you establish a proposal-writing process for your firm, your chances of winning the contracts you pursue will increase. In the current business environment, you need every competitive advantage you can develop.

CHAPTER
≡ Two

9-STEP PROPOSAL PROCESS: AN OVERVIEW

Tracy Masters and Ed Breen met with their boss, Ms. Reiner, to decide how best to respond to the RFP they had received from BioCom. According to the RFP, BioCom wanted an interactive software format that would standardize data from various drug treatment centers. This would make it easier to compare treatment results and enable researchers to develop better treatment protocols.

Breen glanced through the RFP. "I'm not as convinced as Tracy that we should really go after this job. Do we have the technical expertise to design this type of universal software?"

"The vice president of marketing is arranging a teaming agreement with a software firm to give us that expertise," Ms. Reiner said. "Until I hear differently, we have a bid decision. I want you two to concentrate on finding out what the client *really* needs, besides what's stated in the RFP. We need to design a program that addresses all the key aspects of this project."

Masters looked hesitant. "Ms. Reiner, we appreciate your confidence in us, but to be frank, Ed and I are not first-rate writers. We can put together a decent section, but . . ."

"Don't worry. Sid Howland has assigned two writers to work with the proposal team. I'm more concerned about the program design. With the full resources of the company behind this effort, you'll have everything you need to develop a winning proposal."

• • •

Many people make the mistake of believing that the most important consideration in preparing a proposal is how well it is written or how professional it looks. Although good writing and a polished format are important ingredients, the most essential quality of a winning proposal is that it speaks to the client's real needs and sells the client on your company. In some cases, your research may reveal that the real issue is not what is stated in the RFP. You must exercise diplomacy in addressing this area because the client may be invested in solving the problem presented in the RFP. You will have to deal with those expectations while gently leading the client to the topic you want to discuss.

For example, a chain of hardware stores losing business to a rival may believe that the problem is its stores' locations, product lines, demographics, or other factors. In contrast, your research may show the real problem to be lack of customer service—people are switching to the rival chain simply because they experience a higher level of customer satisfaction when they shop there. The rival company's sales staff is courteous and knowledgeable, customer orders are filled promptly, merchandise is guaranteed and, if not satisfactory, replaced or the customer's money refunded. The management is responsive to customer comments and complaints.

Your response to the RFP is to persuade the client tactfully that the real problem is poor customer service. You might say something like the following: "For chain stores, individual store location is often a factor contributing to declining sales. However, industry studies show that two other factors, product quality and customer service, also can seriously affect company revenue. Our initial review of your current situation does not indicate that store location or product quality are the major problems. We propose a broader study that would address customer service as a possible cause for your declining sales." Propose alternative approaches to address the problem and to achieve their goals: "By looking at customer service levels, we can determine what percentage of the decline in sales can be attributed to this problem. We can then devise strategies to correct the situation and to increase sales."

Keep in mind that however you might disagree with what the client believes their problems to be, you must answer those problems in your proposal. Otherwise, it will appear to the client that you have missed the critical issues in the RFP.

The major skills you need to create winning proposals are:

- marketing and sales expertise
- creative and analytical abilities
- decision-making skills
- interpretive skills
- expertise in various subject areas
- communication expertise (writing, client contact, presentation)
- interpersonal skills

In this chapter, we take an overview of the proposal preparation process and see how these skills are applied. The ability to analyze an RFP and devote the necessary time and expertise to prepare a proposal should become a routine part of your company's operations. The preparation process can streamline your efforts each time an RFP comes in or you want to make an unsolicited bid for a job.

9-STEP PROPOSAL PREPARATION AND WRITING PROCESS

Whether you prepare an unsolicited proposal or respond to an RFP the proposal preparation and writing process is fundamentally the same. it can be broken down into nine steps (summarized in Exhibit 2.1):

Exhibit 2.1   9-Step Proposal Preparation Process

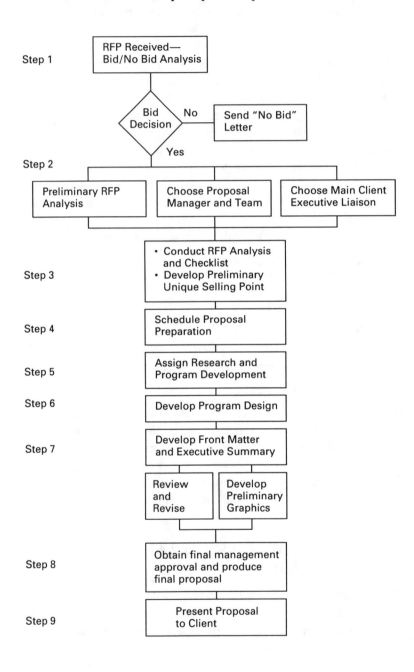

1. Conduct a bid/no-bid analysis/decision.

2. Assign an individual (or a leader and team) responsibility for proposal development. At this point, someone from upper management should be designated as the main client contact throughout the proposal process.

3. Analyze the RFP and develop a checklist. Also develop a preliminary unique selling point (USP) to address the issues in the RFP.

4. Develop a schedule for proposal preparation.

5. Assign and complete research, analysis, program development, and time/cost tasks.

6. Write first draft and develop graphics.

7. Review and revise successive drafts.

8. Obtain final management approval of the proposal, prepare a cover letter or letter of transmittal, executive summary, appendices or attachments, and other details.

9. Present the proposal to the client. If the proposal is not accepted, the client-contact executive follows up to find out why the client chose a competitor's bid.

STEP 1: BID/NO-BID ANALYSIS AND DECISION

The most important management decision a company makes regarding any given project is whether or not to bid for the contract. A proposal represents a significant investment of company resources and should be undertaken only if there is a reasonable chance of winning the contract. Or, you may decide to accept a loss on the job if you wish to establish your company with a client, particularly if the prestige of the client justifies the loss of revenue. The addition of the client's name to your list of completed projects may encourage other clients to hire your company.

There are two parts to this step: an analysis of the RFP and an economic analysis to determine if the potential return outweighs the cost of preparing the proposal and completing the work. Chapter 3 describes the bid/no-bid analysis in detail and shows you how to decline a bid in a way that may generate future business. At the end of this chapter, we have included a list of sources and databases for market research.

STEP 2: THE PROPOSAL TEAM

The proposal team may be composed of only one person or several dozen, depending on the size of your firm and the importance of the project. Chapter 3 explains how to build a good proposal team and outlines the responsibilities of each team member from manager to consultants to support staff.

STEP 3: RFP ANALYSIS

One of the most important tasks in the proposal preparation process is to analyze the RFP to determine what the client may really need in addition to what is stated in the document. This will enable you to develop your unique selling point that can make your firm stand out from the competition. Step 3 is covered in detail in Chapter 4: Finding Your Unique Selling Point. The work done in this step enables you to develop the proposal preparation schedule in Step 4.

STEPS 4 AND 5: PREPARATION SCHEDULE AND ASSIGNMENT OF TASKS

One of the proposal manager's most important jobs is making sure the proposal team meets its deadlines. The manager must plan the effort just like any other company project. (Steps 4 and 5 are covered in more detail in Chapter 4: Finding Your Unique Selling Point.) Exhibit 2.2 presents an example of a simplified schedule that can be adapted for most proposal preparation efforts. The schedule should note the task assigned, the individual (or group and coordinator) responsible for completing the task, due date, and actual dates the work is received. A more sophisticated method available at a fairly low cost is the computerized use of PERT/CPM (Program Evaluation and Review Technique with Critical Path Method) charts. These charts outline the critical steps in the proposal process, which are supported by less critical tasks, and assigns a timeframe to each one.

Exhibit 2.2   Proposal Preparation Schedule

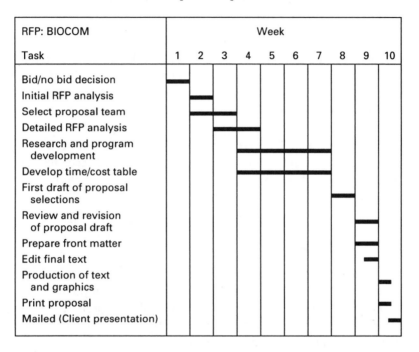

The schedule chart tells the proposal manager quickly whether any part of the team is falling behind schedule or running into difficulties that may require additional staff or resources to handle. This "early warning system" can prevent every manager's nightmare of discovering two weeks before the first draft is due that a major section of the proposal is stalled. Such mistakes not only cost your company time and money—they may cost your firm the project.

STEP 6: DEVELOPMENT OF PROGRAM DESIGN

In Step 6, the proposal manager coordinates all information to develop the final program design. In this step, your firm pinpoints exactly what you will do for the client, how you will do it, and how much time and money it will take to finish the project. This step includes developing time and cost estimates. Program design is the heart of the proposal, and is covered in more detail in Chapter 5: Your Program Design.

STEP 7: DEVELOPMENT OF FRONT MATTER AND EXECUTIVE SUMMARY

Once the first draft of the proposal is complete, top management will review it and usually suggest changes. When they approve the final content, the proposal team will develop the front matter. This step is covered in detail in Chapter 6: Front Matter and Executive Summary.

Front matter for the proposal includes the letter of transmittal, final table of contents and list of illustrations for longer proposals, and the executive summary. The executive summary is a key part of the proposal because it briefly describes the major issues and recommended actions developed by your firm. The executive summary serves as a potent sales piece for your company.

STEP 8: PRODUCING THE PROPOSAL

In Step 8, the manager fathers all proposal sections into one complete document, along with any graphics required. (Proposal production is covered in Chapter 7: Producing Your Proposal.) The proposal usually follows a set format, generally developed by each company. For example, many proposals have a format such as:

TITLE PAGE

COVER LETTER OR LETTER OF TRANSMITTAL

TABLE OF CONTENTS (FOR LARGER PROPOSALS)

LIST OF ILLUSTRATIONS

EXECUTIVE SUMMARY (summarizes main points and recommendations)

I. STATEMENT OF THE CLIENT'S PROBLEM

(An analysis of the client's situation)

II. PROGRAM DESIGN

(Your proposed solution)

   A. TECHNICAL SECTION (technical aspects of the program design)

   B. MANAGEMENT SECTION (description of how the project will be managed and who will make up the management team)

    C. TIME/COST SECTION (estimates of time and cost
       necessary to complete the project, including follow-up)

  III. BIDDER'S EXPERIENCE AND QUALIFICATIONS

    (Why your firm should be hired to do the work; this section
    can include an analysis of your competitors, as well)

  IV. CONCLUSIONS

    (Your final opportunity to sell your proposal to the client,
    including a restatement of your solution and unique selling
    point)

  APPENDICES

    (Staff resumes, recommendations from former clients,
    studies, surveys, contracts, other additional information not
    included in the text)

As you write, be sure that the reading level is appropriate to the client audience—neither too technical nor too simplistic—and that formulas and equations are kept to a minimum (unless they are part of the program design required to sell the proposal).

Once the first draft is completed, the review and revision process begins. Generally, top management will review the draft, often several times, and make suggestions or corrections. Your proposal team is responsible for incorporating these changes into the proposal.

The client may also review a draft of the proposal, depending on the situation. At this point, top management is likely to be in close contact with the managers of the client company. Although management changes may seem arbitrary at times, they are usually based on responses to client concerns or issues that come up in discussions with client management.

Step 8 includes production of the text and illustrations. In this age of desktop publishing, even small companies can produce four-color proposals with impressive charts and pictures. Make sure you involve the production team early in the process to give them enough lead time to create quality illustrations and text design. Even though computerized typesetting and page layout programs make last-minute changes easier, leaving production until the very end increases the chances of new errors being introduced. More than one company has presented a flashy proposal to a company only to discover that the wrong chart or illustration was inserted in a key section. Such simple mistakes reflect badly on your overall credibility.

STEP 9: CLIENT PRESENTATION

Chapter 8 presents strategies for putting together winning client presentations. After all the hard work you have put into your proposal, you don't want to lose out on the final leg by failing to do a quality presentation. Your proposal deserves the best chance for success.

In some cases, you will simply mail your finished proposal to the client, then spend a few nerve-wracking days, weeks, or even months waiting for an answer. If you win the contract, pop the champagne corks and start to work—your proposal effort has been successful.

In other cases, however, writing the proposal is only half the battle. You must also do a client presentation. Here is where your background research on client management and your face-to-face contacts with the client will prove invaluable. You need to know not only how to do a quality presentation but how to anticipate who is likely to give you trouble and how to disarm their objections and soothe their fears. Make no mistake about it—for many managers and workers in the client company, you represent the often unwelcome prospect of change. This is particularly the case if people believe that their jobs may be in jeopardy or that they will be required to learn new procedures.

SUMMARY

This chapter gave you an overview of the 9-step proposal-writing preparation process. The chapters that follow will discuss each step in detail. Chapter 3 presents resources to help you find what you need to know quickly and efficiently. Often, the key to successful proposal preparation is being able to locate the right information at the right time.

CHAPTER
≡THREE

SELECTING THE BID
AND CHOOSING THE
PROPOSAL TEAM

Ms. Reiner met with her boss and owner of the firm, Phillip Vincente, to discuss the BioCom bid and select the proposal team. Mr. Vincente showed her the bid/no-bid analysis data for BioCom and for a second RFP from another healthcare firm, Fairview Hospitals.

Mr. Vincente said, "Your BioCom project almost lost out to the Fairview RFP until I saw the background research on Fairview."

Ms. Reiner paused. "Really? I didn't know the choice was that close. What tipped the balance in favor of BioCom?"

"Fairview has a history of understating their requirements and then loading a lot of extras onto the job and arguing endlessly about minor details. I found out that one of our competitors made only $10,000 on a $600,000 contract with Fairview."

Ms. Reiner breathed more easily. "So BioCom is the better job for us to pursue."

"Absolutely. According to the bid analysis, we have the resources and the expertise, and the return on this project is around 15 percent" Mr. Vincente glanced up at her. "Unless you know of any reason we shouldn't stick with this job."

She shook her head. "There's only one red flag that the bid analysis turned up. We have to make sure that we keep the software development under tight control or we could easily go over budget. If we do a teaming agreement with Software Tracks, as I'm recommending, I'm sure we'll be on target."

"Good. Then let's take a look at who you have in mind for the proposal team."

Ms. Reiner pulled out her file. "For the team coordinators, I've picked Andy Chiang and Barb O'Connell from software development, and Sid Howland from communications. Chiang and O'Connell will develop the technical side of the RFP analysis for us and oversee the software development. The rest of the team is in the file. I've assigned Tracy Masters and Ed Breen to do the background research on BioCom, national drug treatment centers, and firms that are likely to be our strongest competitors for the job."

Mr. Vincente smiled. "Masters and Breen—they're getting to be quite a team." He glanced at the proposal schedule. "You've got some tight deadlines here. Are you sure they can do the research in time?"

"With access to company files and current databases, they should do just fine. In fact, I'd be willing to bet they finish their section of the proposal before anybody else finishes theirs."

•   •   •

It's not uncommon for two or more RFPs to compete for your company's resources in the initial stages of the proposal process. On the surface, the jobs might look equally attractive. The bid/no-bid analysis can help you narrow the field to those jobs that are truly in your company's best interests to pursue. Once you have decided, you'll want to put together the best team to complete the research and writing stages in the most efficient, cost-effective manner possible.

This chapter offers general guidelines on how to select and decline an RFP and how to choose an effective proposal team. These steps are necessary to go on to Step 3 (see Chapter 4), in which you develop a detailed analysis of the RFP to determine the clients' needs and your unique selling point. At the end of this chapter, we also include a section on gathering market research and intelligence not only on the client but on the industry and your major competitors. Collecting information for a successful proposal requires a measure of resourcefulness and computer know-how, but the effort can yield significant rewards if it gives your proposal a winning edge.

STEP 1: BID/NO-BID ANALYSIS AND DECISION

As discussed in Chapter 1, this critical step will determine not only which bids you will pursue but the business considerations that must be weighed for any potential job. In some cases, you may determine that the project may be only marginally profitable—or even represent a potential loss—but that the prestige of the client justifies bidding on the contract.

There are two parts to Step 1. The first is analyzing the RFP for a qualitative fit with your company. Do you have the necessary expertise and resources to complete the project successfully?

The second part is an economic analysis to determine if the potential return will outweigh the cost of preparing this proposal and completing the work. On the basis of these two factors, you can eliminate most RFPs from consideration.

As listed in Chapter 1, the bid decision criteria are as follows:

1. Does the proposal support your total marketing strategy?
2. Is the project within your firm's area of expertise?
3. Do you have a competitive edge over other firms?
4. Do you know the client from previous work?

5. Can you assemble and support an effective proposal team?

6. Do you have a realistic chance of winning the proposal?

The decision-making process is not limited to the initial bid/no-bid choice made when the RFP first arrives. Management also may have to decide whether to pursue the job at several points throughout the process, including after the proposal has been submitted. For example, after one firm submitted a bid to develop hardware for a cellular phone system, three key technical personnel left the firm to join a competitor overseas. Without the proper staff, the company elected to withdraw from the bidding.

Bid/No-Bid Analysis Checklist

As shown in Exhibit 3.1, you can develop a checklist to help you analyze an RFP and reach a bid/no-bid decision. The value of this analysis is not only that it prevents you from spending time and money pursuing jobs you have no chance of winning, but also that it keeps you from winning jobs you can't perform.

Keep in mind that you are responsible for living up to your contract, even if—through inexperience or lack of information—you underbid the cost or underestimate the time it would take to complete a project. Clients can take legal action to force completion of the contract or to obtain monetary damages for nonperformance. The damages can be considerable—even more than the dollar value of the contract. If you insist on taking such chances, you had better keep a good lawyer on retainer.

When You Turn Down an RFP

Should you decide not to bid on a job, you can turn even a rejection of an RFP into a sales piece for your company if you take time to do it properly. Do not simply throw the RFP away or neglect responding to the invitation to bid. Someone thought enough of your company to include it on the bidding list; you can return the favor by being courteous enough to decline the job in writing. This strategy serves three purposes:

- It lets the bidder know you want to be considered for future jobs—or that you are not interested in future bids because the work is outside your area of expertise.

- It gives you a chance to highlight your company's strengths.
- It creates goodwill for your company. The bidder may pass your name on to other firms looking for bids on their work.

Exhibit 3.1   Checklist for RFP Bid/No-Bid Decision

RFP: *Fairvalue Hardware* Date Received: *9/15*			
CRITERIA	YES	NO	UNKNOWN
Supports our marketing strategy	✔		
Project falls in our area of expertise	✔		
Time frame is realistic		✔	
Competitive edge over other firms			✔
RFP part of multiproject work		✔	
. . . etc.			

Generally, letters declining a bid are mailed about one week before the due date for submitting proposals. This gives you time to reconsider your decision should the client make any amendments or time extensions to the RFP.

Exhibit 3.2 provides an example of a letter declining an RFP. Notice that the format of the letter follows a specific pattern, that is, the writer thanks the client for asking the company to submit a proposal; then

Exhibit 3.2   Sample RFP Refusal Letter

Company Logo

July 15, 19—

Mr. J. D. White
Director
South Holland Community Hospital
234 Grande Street
Braniff, OH 34332

Dear Mr. White:

Thank you for inviting us to submit a proposal for your community outreach project. The work is sorely needed in Braniff and the surrounding communities.

We regret to inform you that Hottler and Associates will not be submitting a bid in response to your RFP #3529 titled "Development of Community Outreach Programs at South Holland." We recently lost two of our top consultants to illness and have not yet hired their replacements.

Although we do not feel we can submit a winning proposal for this particular RFP, we would appreciate the opportunity to review other healthcare-related projects in the future. Should you require any assistance in implementing the winning proposal, please do not hesitate to contact us. We have an excellent consultant staff experienced in monitoring the success of new projects.

Sincerely,

Ms. Sandra J. Hottler

Ms. Sandra J. Hottler
President

---

delivers the main point of the letter by stating the reasons for declining the RFP; and finishes by highlighting the company's strengths and expressing a desire to receive other RFPs in the future.

STEP 2: THE PROPOSAL TEAM

In some cases, only one individual needs to be assigned to prepare and write a proposal. But if the job is sizeable or technically complex, you may need to pull together a team. There are three elements to a successful proposal team: a manager to oversee the process, team members with the requisite skills and knowledge, and separate facilities for the team, away from their regular jobs.

The team may also include outside consultants or companies who would work with your firm on the project if you win the job. Team members generally are drawn from various functional specialties such as Research and Development (R & D), Finance, Marketing, etc., to work together toward a common end. To facilitate their work, the team should be given separate facilities away from their usual jobs so they can work without interruptions and distractions.

Besides the proposal manager, various team members can be assigned to coordinate such areas as background and marketing research, competitor information, development of the program plan and budget, and identification of related company expertise and the resumes of staff who will work on the project. The team structure might look like the one in Exhibit 3.3.

Exhibit 3.3   Sample of Team Structure

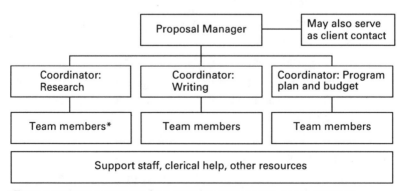

*Team members may come from teaming agreements or subcontracts with other firms as well as in-house staff.

Proposal Manager

The proposal manager provides strong leadership and direction of the team. Even if this person is not an expert in the subject of the RFP, he or she should be knowledgeable enough to help direct and guide the efforts of the team. The individual should have some understanding of the company's computer capabilities and be able to motivate staff and to coordinate and organize the work. It is essential that top management give the manager the necessary authority and support to see the job through to completion. Without top management backing, the proposal manager may not be able to obtain the necessary resources to do the best job. Finally, the manager must know how to set realistic goals to get a high-quality job done on time.

The manager's primary duties include the following:

- If assigned by the company, act as principle client contact and proposal manager. Otherwise, another upper management individual will act as principle client contact and relay client information to the manager.
- Recruit, organize, and direct the proposal planning team. This includes selecting coordinators to direct the activities of various groups involved in research, program development, time/cost analysis, and the like.
- Obtain the services of consultants and cooperating firms (if needed) and define their responsibilities and roles.
- Help the team analyze the RFP to determine the client's needs.
- Establish the proposal-planning schedule and assign tasks to individual members or team task groups.
- Ensure that the team stays on track and within established guidelines and goals.
- Review material submitted by team members.
- Maintain close contact with upper management to report on the team's progress and results and to obtain added assistance when and where it is required.
- Submit the draft proposal to top management.
- Assemble the final proposal and act as liaison between top management, client management, and the proposal team.

- Oversee production and delivery of the printed proposal and follow up to ensure top management and client received it.

The manager's primary job is to build the team and help it stay on target. He or she must encourage communication among members, foster mutual trust, and strengthen the team's commitment to achieve the goals of the proposal effort.

Coordinators

The coordinators, selected by the proposal manager, direct the efforts of their staffs and report to the proposal manager. This structure helps to build strong horizontal linkages between different departments or divisions of a company, which facilitates the proposal process. Generally, each group is responsible for developing and writing a section of the proposal. Coordinators make sure that each group's assigned tasks are completed on time. Their responsibilities include:

- Ensuring that the group understands the overall goals and purpose of the proposal
- Preparing a detailed outline of their proposal section
- Assigning work tasks, setting page limits, and establishing work deadlines
- Using consultants/subcontractors or cooperating organizations as required and integrating their input into the process
- Reviewing drafts and participating in management reviews of draft material
- Incorporating review comments into the final section copy and integrating this copy into the total proposal
- Keeping the proposal manager apprised of the group's progress and requesting assistance as necessary

Team Members

Team members generally are drawn from the ranks of company personnel and are chosen for the specific contributions they can make to proposal preparation. At times, outside consultants or cooperating firms may be required to complete the team roster. You can add outside staff either through consultant agreements or teaming agreements.

Consultant agreements. These agreements are made with individuals who have specialized, often highly technical, expertise. The agreement generally states the conditions under which the consultant will work with your company and a stipulation that he or she will not work for a competing firm during the terms of the agreement. If you win the contract and the consultant is to be included on the project team, this fact should also be stated in the proposal, and the consultant's resume included with other staff members.

It is important not to mislead the client regarding who will make up the staff. Some companies like to parade their experts in order to impress the client, particularly if they can drop the names of some "celebrity" consultants from the industry, academia, or technical fields. If the client awards your firm a contract on the basis of such name-dropping, and later discovers that the consultant will not work on the project, the client might be justified in considering this action fraudulent and might be able to cancel the contract or sue the firm.

Teaming agreement. A teaming agreement can be used to acquire expertise for the proposal preparation and/or to obtain an outside organization's capabilities to work on the project. This is known as a "go-together and split" strategy. Two or more firms join forces to complete a project, then disband when it is over. In this case, the firms should choose only one person to act as principle liaison to the client. Otherwise, the risk of miscommunication between the client and the bidding firms is high.

Your firm may find it necessary to enter into teaming agreements with two or three subcontractors to obtain all the talents and expertise the project may require. The client firm may look more favorably on this combined effort than it would on your firm's efforts alone.

The teaming agreement is a legal contract between your firm and the cooperating organizations. It establishes the conditions and restrictions under which the work will be done and defines the responsibilities of all parties. It is best if the legal staffs of all parties involved work out the details of the agreement to avoid future problems. As in the case of consultants, if cooperating organizations will also work on the client's project, this fact should be highlighted in the proposal.

Proposal Development Specialist

Some firms are turning to proposal development specialists to help them prepare proposals when the company has limited staff or funds to devote to a particular bid. The professional consultants serve either as proposal managers or a one-person team coordinating proposal efforts.

Some large organizations use teams of these specialists on a full-time basis to plan and develop proposals in various areas of client work. Firms that do considerable business with the government, for example, may have proposal specialists who concentrate solely on preparing bids for different government agencies. Because complying with government bid specifications is so complex, and constantly changing, it often requires the full-time effort of a specialist. The effort would be too costly using the company's regular staff. If your firm bids only occasionally on government projects, you should consider using an outside consulting firm to help you prepare the proposal. If the specialists act as proposal managers or coordinators, they will fulfill many of the same responsibilities as on-staff individuals.

WHERE TO LOOK FOR MARKET INFORMATION

Market intelligence for proposals involves not only gathering information on the prospective client, the client's problems as stated in the RFP, and the environment in which they do business, but also on companies that may be bidding against you. In many instances you will have to accomplish your research under tight deadlines, particularly if your company has delayed making a bid decision or has reversed a no-bid decision and is trying for the job after all.

Today the computer has made locating, gathering, and analyzing data infinitely faster and more cost-effective. Even individual consultants who own a good computer and a modem can access databases and conduct in-depth market intelligence searches that in the past only large corporations and libraries could afford.

However, you can begin with other, less exotic sources of information to support your proposal writing. The major sources include:

- The client's RFP, staff, and other materials
- Your own company's knowledge, judgment, and experience

- Market and competitive analysis form
- Your company's library, including swipe files (which contain studies, clippings, annual reports, past proposals, and other data that can be "swiped" for use in current proposals).
- Public information about the client
- Public and specialized databases
- Companies, associations, agencies, or groups specializing in marketing research and analysis

Often, the best place to begin gathering market intelligence is the client. At this point, it is important to have someone from your firm assigned to serve as the principal client contact. This person can go straight to the source and arrange for members of the proposal staff to interview client management and employees. An added bonus of this approach is that you may discover other dimensions to the problem that were not in the RFP or that the client has since uncovered.

The Client's RFP

It is well worth the time it takes to go over the client's RFP in detail. Even the most poorly written proposals, if studied carefully enough, will yield insights into the client's problems. This step will also help you guard against one of the most common—and potentially fatal— mistakes consultants and companies make: jumping to conclusions before they have a thorough understanding of the problem.

Nothing kills a proposal faster than an incomplete grasp of the client's needs. Clients will know immediately if you do not understand their problems; this will render your solutions meaningless and your entire proposal irrelevant.

Learn to read the RFP for what isn't expressly stated as well as for what is. For example, is the problem due to a company's marketing approach or its marketing director? Are there political considerations behind the problem that the client is not stating plainly, but implying? Is there a deliberate gap in the information presented or a personal or corporate bias that may be coloring the situation?

Go over the RFP, using your checklists, until you are satisfied you have gleaned everything you can from it and have identified the major areas that need to be researched. Not only will you have an in-depth understanding of what the client's problems are but will also have ideas about how to address them.

In summary, read the RFP

- for the basic facts regarding the client's situation
- to identify major research areas
- for what isn't said or what may be implied or suggested
- to avoid jumping to conclusions

Client Staff

Conversations with the client are often the second most important source of information after the RFP. If the bidding process permits, schedule appointments to talk with the client's management and staff. You may be able to record these conversations but, if not, be sure to take detailed notes. Memory is notoriously unreliable.

A note of caution: Make sure you have done your homework and read carefully through the RFP before you talk with the client. Your questions should be designed to fill in gaps or obtain more detail on specific areas, not serve as a substitute for reading the RFP. You will not impress a busy executive with your expertise by asking him or her to go over information that you should already know.

Try to talk with more than one level of management or staff. Very often upper management has only part of the picture, particularly where internal operations are concerned. Ask for a tour of the client's operations and branch office or plant sites. You may find that line workers or supervisors have a more accurate knowledge of the cause and cure of many client problems. As more than one consulting company has discovered, a client may spend thousands of dollars for solutions that their own workers have already suggested but that management has discounted or rejected outright.

One major computer chip manufacturer, for example, hired a consulting company to find out why they were experiencing such a high rejection rate of components on the assembly line. The consultant in charge of the project discovered that every line worker knew the answer: faulty epoxy seals. Had they told the process engineers? Yes, he was informed, they had—several times. The engineers refused to listen.

The consultant then asked the engineers why they had dismissed the line workers' reports. He was told quite emphatically that line workers couldn't possibly know anything about component problems! When the consultant pressed them to investigate, the process engineers found to their embarrassment that the line workers were absolutely right. The epoxy seals were not bonding to the silicon base. When the epoxy was changed, the problem disappeared. The consultant recommended a system whereby line worker suggestions were reviewed by a management board.

Tap the knowledge, experience, and judgment of client staff to gain a fuller understanding of the client's situation and possible courses of action. The results of your research can be incorporated into your program design in the proposal. This step can help you tailor your proposal more closely to the needs of individual clients.

Client Materials

Client materials including annual reports, newsletters, brochures, position papers, articles published by company officials, press releases, consumer education pieces, and any other materials that help you understand the mission, products or services, and operating environment of the client. On the surface, these materials will tell you how clients perceive themselves—their corporate culture, position in their industry, relationships with their various markets—and will give you some idea of where they are heading.

To the practiced eye, however, they often reveal far more. Analyze these materials carefully with the following questions in mind.

- Are the materials conservative, daring, innovative, old fashioned?
- What do the materials say about the financial health of the company and how the company is spending its money?
- Is the language focused on management achievements, the company as a whole, the consumer groups they seek to reach, or some other aspect of the business?
- Do they know their markets?
- Are they asking the right questions or offering the best solutions?

- Do they seem to be out of touch with their customers or with their own work force?
- Is there a clash between what the materials say and how the company actually operates?
- Given their resources and potential, is the company aiming too high or too low?

The answers to these questions can give you key insights into the client's problems. For instance, one company made a point of announcing a new customer service package in its brochures, proudly pointing to a new toll-free number that would streamline the handling of customer concerns. In fact, when customers called, the line was always busy, making it difficult to get action on even minor complaints. Sales declined steadily over a six-month period. The company hired a consulting firm to correct the problem. The consultants analyzed the client materials, talked with consumers, and recommended a straightforward solution: the firm should deliver on the promises it made in its brochures—which, in this example, required additional phones and operators.

Keep client materials on file in your library or records department. When you need to prepare a proposal, the materials will be readily available. A staff member can be assigned to update these materials on a regular basis.

Your Own Knowledge, Judgment, and Experience

As a consultant, one of the most valuable assets you have is the perspective you bring to a situation—a perspective that is almost always broader and more inclusive than any individual company possesses. You can draw on your years of experience in a variety of industries, markets, and disciplines or in one or two specific areas to help clients understand their problems in a new way. The market and competitive analysis form (Exhibit 4.2) will also be a source of valuable information in responding to an RFP.

As a result, whenever you receive an RFP, try to see it in terms of the full range of clients you have served, rather than in terms of that particular client. Look at a client's management in terms of the company's background, culture, and style. Are there similarities to other managements you know of that might provide useful clues on how to approach the current client? Is the organization family owned, for example? Or does the management emphasize team concepts, total quality management processes, or a more authoritarian approach? The answers to such questions will help you understand the firm's perspective on its own problems and what sales approach might work best with this particular client.

Also determine if there are solutions that worked in one discipline or field that might apply to the prospective client's situation. For example, could the queuing system you developed to manage a hospital's inventory apply to a retail chain's warehouses? Could the traffic pattern designed for a machine shop work in the greenhouses in a tree nursery?

Draw on the full resources of your company to encourage fresh, creative thinking on all RFPs you consider. This approach takes advantage of the horizontal links in your organization and throws the proposal review process wide open to innovative methods. In one firm, the management regularly asked its various departments to look over all RFPs and offer suggestions. In many instances, this apparently haphazard approach brought more effective solutions more quickly and raised key questions faster than if each department had worked in isolation.

Over the years, your company has developed considerable experience and judgment; put them to work for you on each RFP you receive.

Your Company's Proposal Files and Library

A well-stocked, well-maintained library can be as valuable to you as the fabled treasure of Monte Carlo—and a lot more accessible. Your company should give top priority to updating and improving this library to help you cut down on research time. The computer revolution has made this a far easier task than it was in the past.

Your proposal library should contain at least the following:

- Copies of previous proposals prepared by your firm
- Swipe files
- Competitors' proposals
- Market intelligence books and resources

Copies of Previous Proposals. This resource comes under the heading of "Why reinvent the wheel each time you need a wagon?" In the computer era, you can store copies of company proposals in bound form and on disk, which makes it easy to adapt material or cut and paste sections to be used again.

Keeping copies of proposals—whether or not they were successful in winning contracts—can help the proposal team in several ways. First, the successful proposals serve as models. The team can analyze why these proposals succeeded, how they were organized, and how they were presented. Second, all proposals are likely to contain valuable research and analysis that can save the team time and money. Third, proposals contain graphics, illustrations, tables, and appendices that may be helpful in a current proposal.

Swipe Files. Every company that regularly prepares responses to RFPs should have swipe files. These files include material from previous proposals, studies done on specific topics, information gleaned from newspapers and magazine clippings, informal or formal studies, "for your information" (FYI) items, and any other information deemed worth saving. Files are arranged by topic, company, industry, or other headings and kept in cabinets or on disk. Hard copies of typeset material can be scanned into the computer and included in an electronic file.

Proposal researchers can then access information through index terms or file headings and quickly find what they need. This technique is particularly valuable when time is of the essence, and you need to pull information together quickly on a variety of topics for a proposal.

Copies of Competitors' Proposals. Try to obtain copies of your competitors' proposals, particularly those that won out over yours. If the bidding is open, you can ask the client for copies of competing proposals. At the least, try to find out from the client what key factors influenced the client's decision whether you won or lost the bid.

If you can obtain competitors' proposals, analyze them for information and insights into ways that you can improve your own proposals. The proposals may offer resources or studies that you may have missed in your own research.

It's often true that you learn more from your mistakes than from your successes. By obtaining copies of successful proposals from as many sources as possible, you increase your own chances of winning bids in the future.

Public Data Sources on Clients and Your Competitors

Another quick method of obtaining information on a client or competitor is to search public resources that are easily accessible to any researcher. This step is particularly valuable when the client or competitor is a well-established firm or organization.

The more well-known public resources include:

- Dun & Bradstreet (D & B) reports. These give a brief description and a financial evaluation of the organization or firm.

- Directories such as *Standard & Poor, VALUE LINE, Thomas Register, Directory of Major Public Corporations, Marketing Information.* These directories give a description of the companies, their addresses and telephone numbers, earnings profiles, and names of key management personnel.

- References and books such as *Business Information Desk Reference, Moody's Manuals, Market Share Reporter, Business Rankings Annual, Where to Look,* and *Competitor Intelligence: How to Get It—How to Use It.* Such texts provide additional information on companies and may give you insights into their operations and current issues.

- Journals and periodicals specializing in business reporting, particularly the *Wall Street Journal, Fortune, Investors' Business Daily,* the *New York Times, Forbes, Barron, BusinessWeek,* and specialty publications for various industries. These sources provide more up-to-date information on companies' current conditions and market environment.

In addition, public libraries often have special business research collections to serve the surrounding business community. Such collections can include directories of computer databases, pamphlet files, government publications, and material published by industry associations and organizations. A good research librarian can significantly reduce the time and effort it takes to track down information on a client.

Some companies find it pays to carry or subscribe to these resources in their own libraries. However, if your firm has limited resources and is near a good public library, there is generally no need to duplicate these materials. With today's computer technology, you can request the complete printout of an article from a publication or database. This makes it possible to retrieve magazine and newspaper articles without leaving your desk!

Public and Specialized Databases

Today, using public and specialized online computer databases, one researcher can accomplish what formerly took an entire staff far longer to accomplish. Some of the hardware required for efficient computerized searches include a modem, fax machine, and high-speed printer. The faster the transmission mode, the more efficient your research is likely to be.

Firms can subscribe to databases such as Dialog or CompuServe for a monthly or yearly fee. Public and specialized databases either cover general business information or serve the needs of a particular industry or profession such as banking and finance, health care, food service, government agencies, toxic waste disposal, engineering, and others.

General Databases. A complete list of current databases can be found in such publications as *Directory of Online Databases.* Many are free to users or available for a small fee. This publication contains updated information on nearly 5,000 online databases and is available in the reference section of most public libraries. You might consider keeping such a reference in your company library as well. Make sure you obtain the latest edition, as databases change constantly.

Some of the more common databases used in business proposal research include:

- CITIBASE (1947 to present)—Online service: General Electric Information Services (GEIS); provides financial indicators—U.S. economy, United States/International transactions, population, employment, earnings, etc.
- CITIBASE (weekly updates)—Online service: CompuServe Business Information Service; provides weekly information on U.S. economy.
- DIALOG Information Services—A composite of several hundred databases providing information on various topics and industries, e.g., APTIC (air pollution control), MEDLINE and MESHLINE (medical topics), PSYCH ABSTRACTS, and others.

- DRUG INFORMATION FULLTEXT—Online service: Chemical Information Systems, Inc.; provides full text of 1,400 monographs covering 50,000 commercially available and experimental drugs in the U.S.
- GLOBAL Vantage—Online service: IDD Information Services; offers corporate financial data covering 2,500 U.S. companies and 1,500 companies in 23 other countries.
- HAZARDLINE—Online service: Occupational Health Services; offers information on over 2,000 hazardous substances.
- INFOCHECK—Online service: Pergamon Financial Services; provides business and industry directories.
- Market Potential-SM—Online service: Control Data Corp.; offers demographics and U.S. population figures and marketing consumer surveys.
- MERGERS & ACQUISITIONS—Online service: Securities Data Co., Inc.: provides corporate finance data for U.S. companies.
- MortgageDataR—Online service: Knight-Ridder Money Center; offers information on U.S. securities.
- PATDATA—Online services: BRS (PATS); provides information on any patent registered with the U.S. Patent Office.

This is only a partial list of the many databases available to researchers. Many public libraries today have smaller business libraries within them that cater specifically to business users. Because these libraries seek to attract users, they often obtain the best databases. Ask the reference librarian for help if you don't find what you need.

Setting Up Your Database Search. The secret to any efficient database search is to identify the proper key words, or indexing terms, to use in your search. For example, if you want to locate information on genetically engineered plants, would you look under "plants, genetically engineered," "genetic engineering, plants," or "genetics, engineering, plants"? The right terms in the right order are needed to access information in the databases.

In most instances, each database has a list of indexing terms used to organize information. Make sure you have a copy of such a manual on hand, or ask a computer search expert for help. If you don't have the right key term, you will not be able to access the correct information. It will be like having a treasure chest with no way to open it.

Electronic Bulletin Board System (BBS). Electronic bulletin board systems are the computer equivalent of the company bulletin board where notices, requests, and advertisements are posted. You generally log onto the BBS either through a password, by subscribing to the system, or simply by purchasing the software that lets you into the system.

Once you have access to the bulletin board, you can advertise for the information you want. For example, you can ask for the participation of BBS members in questionnaires or surveys, locate consultants or specialists who may be able to help you with your proposal, gather case histories, and so on.

Using BBS networks can be a quick, inexpensive way to locate information. Your public library or local computer organization may have a directory of BBSs that you can access.

Specialized Research and Information Groups

The computer revolution has spawned a new industry—information management. Specialty firms that do nothing but handle information have sprung up in the past decade or so to help companies find what they need in the avalanche of data that confronts us today. These firms can handle your research requests on everything from how much sugar the average American consumes to the implications of a weak dollar on foreign trade to what price the federal government paid for toilet paper last year.

The public library has directories that list such firms and describe their services and fees. Research and information firms offer services that range from clipping relevant articles on a regular basis, to monitoring specific databases and highlighting information, to preparing formal reports on requested topics.

When you are under a tight deadline to put a proposal together, it may be worth the money to hire one of these specialized research and information groups to do your background work or studies for you. You can then concentrate on developing the program design and recommendations sections of the proposal. In some cases, staff from these groups may be hired as part of the proposal team to work with the client. Such collaborative efforts can enhance your resources without taking away from your current staff.

In addition, some firms hire such groups to do pro-active research, that is, to gather information that is not currently needed but is likely to prove valuable in the future. Such information can then be placed in the swipe files and updated or cut and pasted into a proposal when needed.

Once you have collected and analyzed the information you need, you can begin to finalize your program design and the unique selling point for your proposal.

CHAPTER
≡ FOUR

FINDING YOUR UNIQUE SELLING POINT

After gathering the research data and filling out the analysis checklist, Tracy Masters and Ed Breen met with the rest of the proposal team to analyze the RFP in depth and to develop the unique selling point. Ms. Reiner had included members from the marketing, technical, and software departments who had been assigned to the proposal, and threw the meeting open to anyone who wanted to sit in. To start off, she asked Masters and Breen to share the results of their research.

Breen explained the initial request contained in the RFP.

"BioCom wants to develop a data net software program for drug treatment centers that will codify their results and link all centers around the country via telecommunications. Right now, these centers use a variety of medical formats. This job is tailor-made for us because we have experience in the drug treatment area and in medical software design."

Masters put in, "But so do three of our competitors, so we're hoping one of you has turned up something else in the RFP that we could use as a unique selling point."

Paul Hildago, from Marketing, spoke up. "We've discovered that BioCom has no marketing strategy for the software. For instance, their sales force has a background only in pharmaceuticals. That's fine if they want to sell a medication to help in drug treatment, but they won't be able to talk to the administrators who have to deal with government agencies, the public, self-help groups, and on and on. Also, they have no long-term breakeven analysis to determine how cost-effective it will be to update and sell the software given the rate of technological change and growth of computer information networks like Internet."

Ms. Reiner said, "It looks like we have a two-stage unique selling point: software and marketing strategy. We could show BioCom how to develop the expertise to interface with medical, government, academic, and community groups to gain a significant edge over its competition."

Masters agreed. "With the two-stage solution, BioCom would be a problem solver and advisor to the drug treatment industry. This would make BioCom more recession-proof and less vulnerable to losing clients whenever there was a change in technology or software."

One of the volunteers from Finance spoke up. "Why don't we ask managers at BioCom how they develop their marketing strategy and what kind of training they give their sales force? That way, we could tailor our training methods to mesh with theirs."

Ms. Reiner agreed. "Why don't you come up with a list of questions for the client? All right, people, let's get on this. I want to see the first draft of the program design in one week. Tracy and Brian, work out your assignment and scheduling details with the marketing and technical groups."

•　　•　　•

STEP 3: DETAILED RFP ANALYSIS AND YOUR USP

When your cursory analysis of the RFP and your background research have been completed, you are ready to launch into the detailed RFP analysis to find your unique selling point (USP). The work in this chapter covers Step 3 (detailed analysis), Step 4 (preparation schedule), and Step 5 (assignment of tasks in the proposal writing process). As the firm in the example above learned, part of your solution may be revealed by what *isn't* stated in the RFP. As we mentioned earlier, the gaps you uncover in your analysis can be as important in developing your solution as is the information clearly stated in the RFP.

The unique selling point is how you stand out from the competition. Your analysis of the RFP will help you formulate this strategy, which in turn, will drive the detailed plans for each part of the program design, as described in Chapter 5.

Three Purposes of the Analysis

The RFP analysis step serves three purposes:

- To define the problems and requirements you must address.
- To determine what resources and information you will need to write the proposal.
- To generate the specific tasks that the team groups will be assigned.

For this step, you may want to pull in staff from several departments or areas to help analyze the RFP and develop the main elements of the USP. Often, throwing the process open to this kind of cross-fertilization can be highly effective. You can create an analysis checklist, similar to the bid/no-bid decision checklist in Chapter 3.

RFP Analysis Checklist

The RFP analysis checklist, such as the one illustrated in Exhibit 4.1, provides spaces to list the client's problem or requirement, the RFP page number, the work your team needs to do regarding the problem or requirement, who is assigned the task, the date input is due, the date it is actually delivered, and the page number of your final proposal that responds to the client's original problem or requirement. The team members, coordinators, and proposal manager know by glancing at the checklist exactly where they are in the development process.

Exhibit 4.1   Checklist for RFP Analysis and Task Assignment

RFP: *3577—Biocom*

Problem/RFP Requirements	RFP Pg.#	Input/Task Assignment	Assigned to	Date Due	Date Received	Proposal Prg #	Comments
Loss of Marketshare	5	*Research company,*	*Market research team*	*10/15*	*10/18*	*8*	*Production manager*
		product quality and customers					*strongly resists change*

The checklists can help you identify gaps in your knowledge or database. For example, an agribusiness firm may have perfected a genetically engineered tomato, but if the public is leery of eating this new vegetable, the product could be a financial failure. The proposal researchers would need to learn more about such products, then investigate the best way to persuade customers to accept genetically engineered plants or animals. The results of their research would be incorporated into the program design section of the proposal.

In addition, you can include an edited version of the checklist in your final proposal to give the client a "road map" showing your responses to each of the client's problems and requirements. In this way, you provide a concise summary of the selling points in your proposal. Of course, you should exclude the "comments" column before showing the checklist to the client.

Remember, you need to address all the elements listed in the RFP or you may lose out in the bidding competition. This fact is true even if you discover that some items the client has identified are not related to the actual problem. The client *believes* they are related, and you must discuss them. For example, a client may state that sales decline is due to poor advertising campaigns—but the real reason is poor service. You must still tactfully cover the point the client raised: "Although advertising campaigns have an impact on sales, industry studies show the effect is nearly always short-term and does not account for a persistent decline or uneven pattern in sales. If product quality or customer service is poor, effective advertising will not offset consumers' negative perceptions of a company. In fact, an effective advertising campaign generally raises customers' expectations and decreases their tolerance of poor service or defective merchandise."

Once you have developed a checklist form, the RFP can be analyzed in two stages: an initial quick evaluation and a more detailed analysis.

Quick Evaluation

The initial evaluation can take as little as five or ten minutes to complete, and is one way to obtain an overview of the client's requirements. Your cursory survey can tell you:

- The client's main problem or requirement
- What special resources the contractor requires
- What restrictions are placed on who may bid for the contract
- How much time you have to complete the work

This step can give you a rough idea of what the job entails and what resources you are likely to need to complete the work. You will also be able to spot any major gaps in your knowledge or in your company's expertise and experience. You can then take steps to fill in the gaps, either through research or outside expertise.

Detailed Analysis: Key Questions

Your next step will be to prepare a detailed analysis of the RFP. Some of the key questions you will need to ask are the following:

1. *What is the customer's real versus stated problem?* Clients often confuse symptoms with underlying causes. For example, they may focus on a declining market share rather than on production problems, or on worker morale rather than on their own management policies that may be causing a decline in morale. It is your job to identify the real problem or situation facing the client. Start with the client's view of the problem and look deeper. This is where your background research into the client's history and performance will be invaluable.

2. *What does the client believe is the solution?* Clients frequently believe they know the solution to their own problem. However, if they are not seeing the real situation, then their answers will also be faulty. For example, if the client believes the problem is declining market share, he may feel the answer is more advertising or a better promotional campaign for his products. If the actual problem is production quality, more advertising is not the solution. You will have to listen to the client and persuade him that he will need to overhaul his production facilities to improve product quality. This persuasive task must be done without offending client management (i.e., without implying that management is incompetent, cuts corners for profits, has no sense of the market, etc.). The focus should be on fixing the problem, not assigning the blame.

3. *What experience do you have to handle the client's problem or requirement?* As you go through the RFP, noting problems and potential solutions, you should also be noting what expertise or experience you have to address the issues. In the case of overhauling production facilities, for example, you can note in the checklist who in your company has production experience, or where your gaps in knowledge or experience lie. These gaps will have to be filled in before you submit your final proposal. In this way, you not only get a clear picture of your current resources but also an indication of what resources your company lacks and will need to obtain for the future.

4. *Who is your principal competition? How are they likely to respond to the RFP?* You should always know who your competition is and what they are likely to offer. The RFP analysis checklist can help you identify major competitors. After each client problem or requirement, note which competitor would be able to address that issue and what that competitor's solution may be. In the case of the client with production problems, for example, which company has production experts or experience in the client's line of business? If you don't know, make it a point to find out.

Competitor analysis is a critical component of preparing a winning proposal and should be part of the team's assigned research tasks. Should the client ask you about the capabilities of a rival firm—as a client often will—you will not only be able to discuss that firm but to explain why your company can do a better job. Knowledge of one's competitors can make the difference between winning and losing a job.

The Market and Competitive Analysis Form at the end of this chapter will help you analyze your competition (see Exhibit 4.2 on p. 67). This form provides you with information that will highlight your advantages over your competition and help you pinpoint your competitors' weaknesses, voids, and lack of resources. You will also discover your own weaknesses and problems so that you can devise a strategy to minimize or compensate for them.

As you complete these forms for different firms over time, you will build a file on each competitor and adapt the form as required. This will help you stay informed on the competition's changing position in the marketplace. You can determine if the competition is filling in its gaps and in what direction the management is taking the firm. This information will help your firm position itself to stay ahead of the competition.

The form covers five major areas in evaluating your major competitors and your company: service offerings, company strengths and weaknesses, strategies, market shares, and market segments.

Fill out a questionnaire for each service or product your company may offer. Make sure that department heads and other pertinent staff members receive a completed form and make comments. This leads to the development of action steps to keep your firm competitive. This form represents a partial list of questions you may find useful. You may want to customize the list of questions to meet your exact needs.*

5. *Will the preparation effort require any demonstrations, benchmark tests, or other preliminary work?* In some cases, the RFP will indicate a need for you to develop some form of demonstration or benchmark test to convince the client that your firm is capable of doing the work. For example, you may need to demonstrate how product quality has slipped or how a manufacturing process has become inefficient. Such demonstrations or tests will require time to develop. You will need to indicate on the checklist who will be assigned the task and the estimated time required.

   A word of caution: Make sure your demonstration or test focuses on defining and clarifying the problem as the client perceives it and not as you perceive it. Nor should the demonstration or test inadvertently tell the client how to solve the problem. Otherwise, you will supply the client with an answer at your expense.

6. *Who in the client's organization is likely to support or oppose your proposal?* The checklist can also help you note the political climate in a client's organization. Who are the decision makers likely to be? Are there any managers or executives who may present obstacles? What is the philosophy of top management? For example, if production problems are part of a client's situation, is the director of production likely to support or resist proposed changes in operation?

   Your background research should include an analysis of the organizational and political situation in the client's company. At the least, you should be able to determine the power structure and identify the major decision makers in the company who may have the authority to approve or reject your proposal. This information can help you tailor your

---

* If you need additional information on interpreting your results, see Hamper and Baugh, *Strategic Market Planning,* NTC Publishing Group, 1990.

presentation to recognize and overcome the objections of some managers or executives and to ensure that your proposal has a greater chance of success.

7. *What is your unique selling point likely to be?* At this point, you probably will not know for certain what program or unique selling point you will have to offer the client. However, you may have some indications in both areas and should note any ideas or insights on the checklist.

   For example, if the client's manufacturing process needs improving, your unique selling point may be a specific process or series of work flow steps that your company has developed or that you have discovered in your industry research. You may not know at this stage whether the process will work for the client, but it could be the edge you need. By jotting down your ideas or insights, you keep a record of all ideas for further development and for future RFPs.

   These notes also may serve as the basis for the first rough draft of the proposal. The next stage would be a more complete draft that could be submitted to upper management for review. You may go through several drafts before producing the final version.

8. *Who will form the project team?* One of the key steps in preparation is selecting the right personnel to do the job for the client. At this stage, you can begin updating resumes of key people who are likely to form your project team. Resumes should be slanted toward the client's needs, highlighting your staff's experience, knowledge, or expertise in areas that address the client's problem or situation. Your company should keep resumes in computer files that can be quickly updated and tailored to each proposal (see sample resumes in Appendix C).

9. *What are your company's experience and qualifications for the job?* When listing client problems or requirements in the checklist, you can also note where your firm has the most experience or has done previous work for other companies. This step will help you prepare the section on your company's qualifications. This item can be seen as a resume for your company, highlighting your company's previous experience in the client's field, prior contracts, and types of work undertaken.

This information should be on computer so that the proposal manager can update and tailor it for each proposal.

10. *How much will the proposal effort cost your firm?* The time and staff costs of preparing proposals should be charged to a separate account. The estimates should include such items as writing, production, and printing expenses, as well as travel, staff salaries, and research costs. The easiest way to estimate how much it will cost your firm to prepare a proposal is to work backward from the expected value of the current contract.

These questions will help focus your initial analysis and get you to think from the client's point of view right away.

Asking the Client for Information

You also can use these questions as a starting point to generate more focused and detailed questions for the client. Not all the information you need will be in the RFP; also, the writer may have been unclear about certain specifications or conditions, or there may be gaps in the RFP you need to fill in.

Make sure you protect your own interests when submitting questions. Ask the client if all bidders will see lists of one another's questions. If so, make sure you are not giving away proprietary information or tipping your hand to your competitors. If you have questions you'd like the client to answer that involve revealing a key piece of your solution or some other sensitive material, submit these questions separately in a sealed envelope and request a private meeting with the client to discuss them. You may even want the client to sign a propriety information note that binds them not to reveal the content of your questions.

Once you have obtained the information you need, you can begin to focus on your solution and unique selling point.

A Question of Value

When clients ask for proposals, they are looking for a customized service tailored to their particular needs and goals, and they want the highest value for their money. The unique selling point that you develop has to deliver not only in terms of performance but in terms of this type of value. Keep in mind that an *acceptable* proposal is not enough. Every one of your competitors may turn in an acceptable proposal. A *winning* proposal must go one step further and do *all* of the following to provide the highest value for the client's dollar:

- Show that you understand the client's problems better than the client does.

- Present a detailed, achievable plan showing how you will solve the client's problem within the constraints of the RFP.

- Show evidence that your firm is highly qualified to implement the plan.

- Meet all RFP requirements, including delivering the proposal to the client *before* the stated deadline.

- Sell the client on the credibility of your plan and your firm. Your proposal must create absolute confidence that your firm can deliver the promised service or product.

The information from your background research will prove invaluable at this point. Remember, your background research should cover the following:

- The topic of the RFP, background of the project, and the client's history, organization, and budget for the project.

- The competition's strengths and weaknesses regarding the RFP topic and compared with your firm. For example, your competition may be strong in software programming in general, but less experienced than your firm in a specific type of software programming. This fact gives you an advantage that can be a selling factor to the client.

- The target market for the RFP product. In the sample case, for instance, the product is the software and the marketing strategy. The target market is BioCom and the administrators and staff of innovative drug treatment programs. Your company needs to know who besides the client will receive the proposal product or service.

Client's Needs and Wants

Using this background research, the proposal team should be able to generate a prioritized list of the client's needs and wants. Exhibit 4.3, Client's Needs/Wants Analysis Form, will help you determine these needs/wants, your firm's response to each one, your competitor's likely response to each, and a comment section where you can interpret the responses. For BioCom, Andover Medical Consultants' list might read as follows:

1. Software program to format medical data to permit easy access, analysis, and transmission to computer systems of other drug treatment centers

2. Extensive knowledge of drug treatment programs and their administrators and staff

3. Software that will be easy to update, highly reliable and user-friendly, and adaptable to changes in technology

4. Reasonable development time and cost

5. Sales and marketing expertise to market product.

When filling out the form, be ruthlessly honest. For example, if you have problems with cost overruns or take longer to develop a product than your competitors, admit it. Only you and your staff will see the list, so there is no point in dodging the truth. If you cannot base your proposal on reality, you are better off not trying for the job.

Once all the responses have been interpreted, look at the form in its entirety and summarize its contents. This will enable you to develop a proposal that will address all of the client's needs/wants, which will help give you an edge over your competitors.

After you have finished the form, take time to re-analyze what you believe your competitors' likely responses will be. The rationale for doing the analysis a second time is simple: some managers have a tendency to minimize their competitors' strengths and exaggerate their weaknesses to the point where the responses are distorted. Such a tendency will only reduce your chances of winning the bid. You may have to use your intuition on some of the items, but you probably know your competition better than you think you do.

This form, when completed, will show you where you have a competitive advantage or disadvantage. The areas of clear advantage generally form the basis of your unique selling point. For Andover Medical Consultants, the USP is twofold: create the best software program and help BioCom develop a sales and marketing strategy.

Exhibit 4.3   Client's Needs/Wants Analysis Form

Client: _Biocom_   Date: __8/15__
                            Proposal Mgr: _Ms. Reiner_

1) Client's Need/Want
   Software program to format medical data to permit easy access, analysis, and transmission to computer systems of other drug treatment centers.

   Our Firm's Response

   _____
   _____
   _____

   Competitor's Likely Response

   _____
   _____
   _____

   Comments

   _____
   _____
   _____

2) Client's Need/Want
   Extensive knowledge of drug treatment programs and their administrators and staff.

   Our Firm's Response

   _____
   _____
   _____

   Competitor's Likely Response

   _____
   _____
   _____

   (Continued)

Comments

_____

_____

_____

3) Client's Need/Want

Software that will be easy to update, highly reliable, and user-friendly, and adaptable to change in technology.

Our Firm's Response

_____

_____

_____

Competitor's Likely Response

_____

_____

_____

Comments

_____

_____

_____

4) Client's Need/Want

Reasonable development time and cost.

Our Firm's Response

_____

_____

_____

Competitor's Likely Response

_____

_____

_____

Comments

_____

_____

_____

5) Client's Need/Want

   Sales and marketing expertise to market product.

   Our Firm's Response

   _____

   _____

   _____

   Competitor's Likely Response

   _____

   _____

   _____

   Comments

   _____

   _____

   _____

   Final Summary

   _____

   _____

   _____

   _____

   _____

   _____

   _____

   _____

   _____

Value-Added Elements

While developing your USP strategy, keep in mind that you may be able to add features as you go along. This value-added approach enables you to respond to information you gain from the client or from additional research. You might use a form to record your ideas, such as the one shown in Exhibit 4.4. For instance, Andover's sales and marketing strategy for BioCom might include any or all of the following elements:

- Education and training for sales staff

- Financial breakeven costing methods

- Projections for upcoming changes in medical computer technology and software

- Methods for analyzing drug treatment operations and pinpoint opportunities for software upgrades

- Methods for interfacing with other medical data networks to improve the transmission and sharing of information

Exhibit 4.4   Value-Added Elements Form

Instructions:

1. Fill in the information at the top of the form: client, date, proposal manager, and names of your primary competitors in the bidding process.

2. After each element in the list, analyze your firm compared to your competitor(s). Use a "+" sign to indicate an advantage your firm possesses; a "0" when you and the competition are equal; and a "−" to indicate when your firm is at a disadvantage compared to the competitors. You should customize the list for your particular situation.

3. Use the comments section to note whether an element adds to the value of your plan, indicates a strength or weakness of your firm or your competitors, or reveals other information that may be useful in developing the unique selling point.

(Continued)

Value-Added Elements Form

Client: _BioCom_

Date: _8/21_

Proposal Mgr.: _Ms. Reiner_

Element	Your Firm	Competitor 1	Competitor 2	Comments
1) Service				
2) Training				
3) Technical support				
4) Software upgrades				
5) Geographic coverage				
6) Pricing				
7) Service line breadth				
8) Service differentiation				
9) Employees backgrounds				
10) Service quality				
11) Compatibility				
12) Breadth of service application				

Comments Summary

_____

_____

_____

_____

Each element should be considered part of the entire strategy, much like modular units are part of a whole. This modular approach to building in value and value-added elements makes your solution more flexible and allows you to tailor it more precisely to the client's needs. For example, Andover Medical Consultants may be able to include some of the following value-added items to its proposal to highlight the company's unique strengths:

- Demonstrate high service levels at no additional cost.
- Offer computer software upgrades at a nominal fee.
- Provide a special technical support telephone number for any questions client staff may have.
- Provide different levels of training to executives, middle management, supervisors.
- Show that Andover's geographic coverage of BioCom's customers is superior to the competition's and that Andover can provide superior service should BioCom expand their operations.

STEP 4: PREPARATION SCHEDULE

Once you have identified the main elements in your unique selling point strategy, you can begin to fill in the proposal-writing schedule (see Exhibit 4.5). This schedule establishes specific due dates for each task as well as for the first drafts of the technical, management, and time/cost sections of the proposal, the front matter, and the executive summary. Everyone on the proposal-writing team should know the deadlines for their sections of the proposal, the date the first draft of the complete document is to be assembled, and the date the document is to be turned over to management for review.

STEP 5: ASSIGNMENT OF TASKS

Now that you have a concrete idea of your timelines, you can decide on the most effective and efficient assignment of tasks. In some cases, the person who has an idea is not the best person to develop it or write about it. If you are in charge of the proposal-writing process, part of your job is to know what tasks to delegate to which people. Exhibit 4.5 shows a sample writing assignment schedule form.

Page _____ of _____

Exhibit 4.5   Form for Writing Assignments

RFP Page Nos.	Proposal Page Nos.	Topic or Section	Date Due	Date Received	First Review	Final Review	Writer	Comments

In addition to making due dates very clear, it's a good idea to require routine progress reports from your proposal-writing staff. This approach has two major advantages. First, it allows you to detect quickly if someone is going off course. Even the best researchers and writers can occasionally get sidetracked by an attractive but inappropriate idea or product. The sooner you catch their mistake, the better your chances of keeping the proposal on course and on schedule.

The second benefit of routine progress reports is that it prevents people from procrastinating on their assignments. If they must report regularly to you, they will have to keep at the job each day or explain to you why they are not working on the proposal. If you see a person is not up to his assigned task, you can replace him early in the process.

Now you are ready to develop strategies for each of the three sections in your program design. Chapter 5 presents a detailed outline for each section, what each contains, and who in the client organization will read which sections. Before moving on to Chapter 5, you may want to look over the Market and Competitive Analysis Form (Exhibit 4.2) following this page.

Exhibit 4.2   Market and Competitive Analysis Form

Instructions:

1. Complete the information at the top of the form: competitor names, date, and the proposal manager responsible for the project.

2. In section A, answer the questions about you and your competitors in the context of your respective situations. Use a "+" sign to indicate an advantage that your firm possesses; a "0" to indicate that you and a competitor are equal in this area; and a "–" sign to indicate a disadvantage or gap your firm possesses versus the competition.

3. In section B, answer the questions from the competitor's viewpoint, unless the question specifically asks you to compare the competitor's offering with your service.

4. In section C, fill in the summary of your findings.

Answer as many questions as you can. Whenever possible, research the questions you cannot answer using your current knowledge. The more high-quality answers you generate, the more information you will have to prepare a winning proposal. And remember: What you *don't* know about your competitors can be as critical as what you *do* know. These voids in your knowledge point out where you are vulnerable to competition and reveal potential problems and opportunities for your firm.

Once the form is completed to the best of your ability, summarize your findings within the context of the entire form. This method allows you to conduct both a micro and macro analysis. Companies often make the mistake of looking at only one question at a time. You need to correlate the questions to obtain the best possible view of each competitor and your own firm.

(Continued)

Market/Competitive Analysis Form

Client: _____

Competitor's Names: _____

_____

Date: _____

Proposal Mgr.:

_____

Section A:

	Our Firm	Competitor 1	2
1. Product differentiation from competitor's offerings.			
2. Cyclicality of market segment (i.e., constant, seasonal, etc.).			
3. Skills of the firms (all aspects).			
4. Product quality/service levels perceived by customers.			
5. Flexibility of pricing structure.			
6. Price competitiveness.			
7. Barriers to entry.			
8. Variety of applications and features.			
9. Regulatory climate.			
10. Risk in market segment.			
11. Required investment to stay competitive.			
12. Estimated profit margin ($).			
13. Estimated profit margin (%).			
14. Supplier power.			
15. Buyer power.			

Client: _____

Section B

Competitor A: _____

1. Does this firm offer complementary services?

   Their offering(s)   Your service equivalent

   _____   _____

   _____   _____

   _____   _____

2. Do they have technological advantages over our products?

   Their offering(s)   Your service equivalent
   and advantages

   _____   _____

   _____   _____

   _____   _____

3. Do they add value to their services over ours?

   Their offering and   Your service equivalent
   its added value

   _____   _____

   _____   _____

   _____   _____

4. What geographic area or niche are they targeting as their market?

   List niches and service   Your service equivalent
   offering in each

   _____   _____

   _____   _____

   _____   _____

5. Is their pricing strategy by individual service, total package, or both?

   Describe their pricing strategy

   _____

   _____

   _____

(Continued)

6. What percent have they gone above or below the price of their service to make a sale?

   Product offering and
   price variance

   Your service equivalent

   _____   _____
   _____   _____
   _____   _____

7. Do you feel this firm is cutting prices to increase bid acceptances for the long run or the short run?

   Their service   Method of price cutting

   _____   _____
   _____   _____
   _____   _____

8. What customer voids do their services fill that your service(s) do not?

   Competitor's service(s)   Associated customer
                                     voids

   _____   _____
   _____   _____
   _____   _____

9. What is their geographic coverage for their services (i.e., local, regional, national, international, etc.)?

   _____
   _____

10. Do customers perceive this firm's products as technologically superior or inferior to yours?

   _____
   _____
   _____

11. What service applications does this firm have above or below your offerings?

   _____
   _____
   _____

12. List specific target markets/segments/industries for each competitor service offered.

Service   Target market/segment/
                                 industry

_____   _____

_____   _____

_____   _____

13. What specific background advantages or disadvantages do their employees have, compared to your firm's employees (e.g., degrees, experience, personal contacts)?

Their advantages   Their disadvantages

_____   _____

_____   _____

_____   _____

14. Compared to your firm, what technological advantages and disadvantages do they demonstrate?

_____

_____

_____

Client: _____

Section C

Summary

_____

_____

_____

_____

_____

_____

_____

_____

CHAPTER

≡FIVE

DEVELOPING YOUR PROGRAM DESIGN

Ms. Reiner met with the proposal team to go over the development of the program design.

"We have a two-part approach to BioCom's problem: develop the software and give them a marketing strategy. Now we need to nail down the program design and get the technical, management, and time/cost sections on paper. BioCom has to know exactly what we're going to do, how we're going to do it, and how much time and money it will take to finish the job."

She consulted her notepad. "The software designers are doing the technical section, and Finance will do the time/cost calculations. Tracy and Brian, I'm giving you the management section. We have the information we need from the client about how they develop their marketing strategy and train their sales force."

Tracy spoke up. "From what you've said about BioCom's data processing director, if we get the project, we'll need to have someone in charge who can keep the work on schedule. I understand their director is more the engineering type who gets lost in detail."

Ms. Reiner nodded. "The last team project he headed up was six weeks overdue. I'd recommend that our production director, Brad Carlos, be put in charge of the team. I'll have to do some fancy diplomatic work to get BioCom to agree to this, but I think Liz Everett, their operations officer, knows the problem."

Ed Breen put in, "Tracy and I will take a look at some of the swipe files—we'll have to show BioCom that Andover has the necessary management experience to organize a project like this. We'll need to know which of our consultants will be included in the proposal as project team members so we can pull their resumes."

Ms. Reiner made a note. "I'll get back to you on that by Friday. I'm talking with Art Delos this afternoon about who should be on the team. All right, what about time and cost calculations?"

One of the finance team members raised his hand. "From what BioCom said in its proposal, it wants a cost breakdown by major expense category. Also, general and administrative costs shouldn't be more than 15 percent of the total. We figure that with a 10 percent cost overrun built in, we can achieve about a 5 percent profit margin on this project."

"Provided nothing goes seriously wrong," Ms. Reiner said.

"Yes, provided nothing goes seriously wrong."

Ms. Reiner turned to the software design team. "Nothing is going to go seriously wrong, is it?"

The software team leader shook her head amid the general laughter. "Not if we have anything to say about it. We'll work with Finance on the time schedule. Based on prior work, I think we can have the software up and running in about six weeks. It's similar to the job we did for the pharmaceutical industry last year. Oh, and we'll talk to the legal department about putting the nondisclosure statement together."

Ms. Reiner opened her project calendar. "All right, let's set due dates. I want the technical, management, and time/cost sections by Wednesday of next week. That gives you all six days. Any problems with that?"

She looked around the table. The team members glanced at each other. No one appeared to have a problem with that.

•   •   •

STEP 6: PROGRAM DESIGN—THE HEART OF YOUR PROPOSAL

The service or product your firm offers the client represents your unique selling point (USP) in the proposal and must be expressed in the form of a program design. The design has several features:

- It identifies the real problem or need in the RFP and discusses it from the client's point of view. Whether this is simply the stated problem or a problem that your research reveals, you must cover all elements in the RFP.

- It tells the client *what* your company will do, by describing the approach you will take to address the problem(s).

- It tells the client *how* your company will do the job, by describing in more detail the services that your company will provide to meet the client's needs.

- It describes the staffing, time, and cost requirements needed to complete the job. The client will then have a good idea *who* will do the work, *how long* it will take, and *how much* it will cost.

THREE PARTS OF THE PROGRAM DESIGN

The technical section, management section, and staffing/time/cost section each contributes to the winning proposal. Pay careful attention to the details in each one. It won't matter if you have an outstanding technical strategy if your management strategy is lacking. This gap tells the client you may know *what* to do but not *how to get it done.* Many proposals are weak in this area. Keep in mind that you must sell the client on your *firm,* not just on your ideas.

Technical Section

The technical section has three goals:

- To show the client that your product or service can meet the RFP requirements
- To demonstrate your understanding of the client's requirements and your firm's capacity to anticipate and resolve problems and to provide a workable solution
- To show the client you can perform the work required

The technical strategy in this section should convince the client that you have a superior grasp of the problems stated in the RFP and have devised a superior solution. The technical strategy may pick up other items from the general needs/wants list prepared earlier. In this way, you begin to build a coordinated strategy that ties all three sections together and reinforces your overall differentiation strategy.

For example, the firm in the sample case may build into their software program a few features that will make it easier to market to administrators. These features could include ways to correlate third-party payments or incorporate periodic changes in Medicare diagnostic and treatment codes. Such detailed strategies can work together to meet your customer's needs/wants and to sell your proposal.

It is critical that the detailed strategy for this section focus on the client's primary concern. For example, does the client want

- a more sophisticated technical solution?
- greater safety than other solutions?

- increased productivity over other solutions?
- easier operation?
- quicker delivery?
- more versatility?
- a combination of these elements?

Your background research should help you discover the client's primary concern. Make sure you can state the concern clearly in one or two sentences, for example, "The client wants a software program that will make formatting data easier and faster. This strategy includes other features such as compatibility with different systems, ease of operation, increase in productivity, and greater facility in communicating with other treatment centers."

Avoid the temptation to develop more than one technical strategy in a proposal. Generally, you need to focus on one main strategy rather than scatter your forces trying to develop two or more. However, you may have one or two minor strategies that link to the main strategy. For example, if improving customer service is the main strategy, a minor strategy might be developing special promotions and customer giveaways to support the main focus of the proposal.

Who Reads the Technical Section? In general, the people who developed the RFP and who are in charge of the project will read and evaluate the technical section. Their primary focus will be on the technical details of your proposed solution, and they may not have a marketing or sales perspective. However, they should be able to understand the marketing and sales implications of your technical product or service as well as pricing models and market strategies.

Keep in mind that although your readers will be competent in their individual fields, they may not be experts in your technology. When writing the technical section, don't assume a level of knowledge about your work that the readers may not have. Be careful to explain terms, concepts, processes, and any software/hardware that is unique to your company, field, or industry. You do not need to talk down to your audience, but take into consideration the readers' point of view when you write the proposal. Your background research should tell you the level of knowledge and expertise of those who will be evaluating the technical section. Do not make any assumptions without doing research.

How Should It Look? Although the format will vary somewhat depending on the RFP requirement, a technical section generally has the following:

- Section Overview—introduces the content of the technical section and acts as a roadmap to help readers find specific topics in the text
- Introduction—presents your understanding and interpretation of the client's problem
- Solution—explains your approach to the problem—why you developed the solution that you did, and the main features of the solution
- Product or service description—provides additional details of the product or service your solution offers the client
- Installation and implementation plan—outlines how you will install any necessary equipment or processes and how you will measure whether they are implemented and used successfully
- Project organization and key project staff information—describes how the project will be organized and introduces the key personnel from your firm who will work with the client

In addition to the information above, many technical sections also include a discussion of assumptions made during the proposal-writing process. In some cases, an RFP has insufficient information or the client may not know the answers to your questions, and your background research does not provide the missing data. In such instances, you may need to make certain assumptions to fill in the gaps. This is a standard method of operation to keep working on your proposal even when you do not have all the information you need.

Assumptions should be based on your firm's expertise in the client's problem area and carefully supported and documented in your proposal so the client knows why you made the assumptions and on what they were based.

Take care to avoid the trap of "assuming away" problems to meet your needs. If you learn that a client manager has objections to your program design, for example, don't assume that you will be able to answer whatever questions he or she may raise. You could find out the hard way—in the client presentation—that you are unprepared.

Nondisclosure Statement. At times, you may need to go into some detail in the technical section. To prevent the client, or a competitor, from using your proprietary information, you can include a *nondisclosure statement* with the proposal (see Exhibit 5.1). You will need to consult your legal department or a lawyer about the proper wording of the statement.

A nondisclosure statement can appear in several forms. It may be a statement included on the title page and every page thereafter of the proposal. It also can be placed on all preparation materials you develop within your firm. At times, a nondisclosure statement is a signed agreement between your company and the client that forbids the client to disclose or reveal to anyone outside of the project the information contained in your proposal or learned through discussions with you.

If you have any doubt about how the client will handle material you include in your technical section, have them sign a nondisclosure statement. If they refuse to do so, you must then assess the risk/benefit of submitting the proposal and possibly losing proprietary information.

Management Section

The management section has two goals:

- To show the client that your firm has the experience, personnel, and resources needed to do the work you describe in your proposal.
- To demonstrate your firm's understanding of the details of the project, such as managing the project, installing equipment or processes, training client personnel, devising test procedures, and monitoring results.

You may not always have a separate management section. Depending on the RFP, you may include management strategy or information about your firm in the technical section. Some RFPs, for example, request information about a firm's management, resources, and experience but not about managerial function such as installation, testing, monitoring, etc. For the purposes of this chapter, however, we are assuming that you need to write a separate management section in response to an RFP.

Exhibit 5.1   Nondisclosure Statements

1. *Statement on Company Materials*

   PRIVATE

   The information contained herein should not be disclosed to unauthorized persons. It is meant solely for the use of authorized Andover employees.

2. *Statement Included on Company Proposal*

   Attached is the April 19— BioCom plan. This binder is the responsibility of J.R. Smith and is not to be reproduced. It contains certain private and confidential data concerning the BioCom plan.

3. *Statement to be Signed by Client Company*

   NONDISCLOSURE STATEMENT

   BioCom agrees to keep all information contained in this proposal confidential. It is understood that the proposal contains proprietary information developed by Andover Medical Consultants specifically for BioCom and that this material is not to be reproduced nor disclosed to any unauthorized personnel.

Signed _____

Date _____

The management strategy tells the client that your company will be able to implement the solution—and no doubt about it! All too often, however, management is one of the most neglected areas in proposal planning.

Why? Often, the answer is surprisingly simple: the proposal team is focused on developing a product or service and on the nuts and bolts of who will do the job, how long it will take, and how much it will cost. As a result, the management strategy has no champion. More often than not, at the last moment, someone hastily writes a few pages, slaps them into the proposal, and—voila!—a "management plan."

The management strategy is important for two reasons: (1) it can be another way to sell your firm and differentiate yourself from the competition and (2) it shows the client *how* you intend to get the job done. Your management strategy must support the technical strategy and complement the proposals-differentiation strategy. You can use this section to stress your competence and unique selling point in various ways. Some typical management strategies include:

- Stressing superior management experience in producing similar products or services in the past
- Emphasizing that top management will have direct control of the project
- Demonstrating that you have exceptionally qualified personnel who will work on the client's project
- Convincing the client you can provide superior quality assurance during each phase of the project
- Stressing your manager's expertise in implementation and follow-through. The work doesn't end with the development of a product or service; you will ensure that the client is satisfied with how it performs in operation.

Developing this section forces you to think through the "best case/worse case" scenarios in terms of possible delays, setbacks, conflicts, and misunderstandings. It gives you a chance to ask "What if?" questions and create contingency plans to hold in reserve should your original management plan run into problems. For instance, what if a supplier can't meet a delivery date, or a software program requires more than the usual debugging, or you lose a key staff member in the midst of the project? Devising contingency plans for these situations can save you a great deal of time, embarrassment, and financial loss in the future.

Generally, contingency plans are not written into the proposal but kept in a separate file. All the client knows is that you have thought through a solid management plan.

In some cases, the management strategy can be the section where you stand out from the competition. Remember, the fundamental goal of a proposal is to sell your firm to the client. In some instances, your technical and cost sections may be similar to other proposals the client receives; a well-thought-out management strategy could make the difference between success and failure.

Who Reads the Management Strategy Section? Generally, the same people who read the technical section will evaluate the management section. Once you have convinced the client about *what* you can do, you must convince them that you know *how* to do it. As a result, the technical and management sections must be written so they have a consistent theme.

For example, if the technical section emphasizes how easily a new billing program can be integrated into the client's computer system, the management section should not contain an elaborate, complex plan to oversee implementation and monitoring of the program. The client will naturally want to know: If the process is so easy, why does it take so much time and effort to install and run it? The client may think twice about awarding you the job. If you claim in the technical section that your solution is easy to install and use, your management section must show a clear, straightforward implementation plan. Your proposal must be consistent in order to present a convincing case.

How Should It Look? There are several ways to organize a management section. At the least it should provide an introduction to the management plan; an outline of your firm's capabilities; which personnel from your firm will be responsible for overseeing the project and for implementation, training, and monitoring; and what the client's responsibilities are. A suggested outline might look like the following:

1. Introduction—an overview of the entire section.

2. Project management approach—a description of the approach that you feel will best direct the project successfully, whether team or project management, co-management with client personnel, or some other approach.

3. Project organization and responsibilities—how the project stages and tasks will be organized and who will be responsible for accomplishing each stage or task.

4. Management of subcontractors—in some cases, part of the project may need to be completed by subcontractors. These vendors will require close supervision. You may or may not want to mention the need for subcontractors in the proposal. This is a decision that will have to be made on a case-by-case basis. Some clients may consider the use of subcontractors to be an indication that your firm is incapable of doing the job. Others

may see it as a sign of resourcefulness. Your knowledge of the client will guide you in this matter.

5. Project schedules—a critical management task to keep the project on track. The schedules must reflect realistic estimates based on your knowledge of your firm, experience with similar projects, and client resources.

6. Implementation, training, testing, and monitoring—this stage is critical to the ongoing success of the project. The client must be satisfied with the initial solution as well as the long-term performance of that solution. The management plan must include provisions for training personnel and for testing and monitoring the product or service over a set period, usually three to six months, but in some cases up to a year or more.

7. Staff resumes, references from other clients, and a history or other pertinent information about your firm.

Boilerplate Files. Several items in the management section can be prepared from boilerplate files. These are resumes, company descriptions, client references, and other material that will be used over and over in your proposals (see sample boilerplate resumes in Appendix C). Once on computer, the files can be adapted to the requirements of each RFP. For example, if your staff members have expertise in telecommunications, programming, and marketing, you can tailor their resumes to each client. For a client looking to develop a cable marketing service, you would stress your staff's and your firm's telecommunications and marketing expertise and prior work on related projects.

Boilerplate files can help to streamline the proposal-writing process. With the computing power available to even one-person consulting firms, boilerplate files are easy for anyone to create. Some of the files you should keep on computer include:

- Project management approach. Over time, you may discover that a particular management approach works well for your firm. This file could contain a general description of that approach, including a statement of work, a management plan, and work schedules.

- Organization charts, flow charts, other exhibit materials. You may use organization or flow charts to show your firm's structure and method of operation, how your project management system works, or any other topic you routinely illustrate in an RFP. With computer graphics, you can change, adapt, or recreate these illustrations with ease. (See Chapter 7: Producing Your Proposal.)

- Staff resumes. You may want to have several versions of all staff members' resumes available, so you can stress different skills and experience they have in different areas. Resumes should be kept on senior management staff, project managers, technical personnel, and product developers.

- Contracts. This file could include standard forms for agreements you make with subcontractors, service companies, outside consultants, suppliers, team agreements, and the like.

- Training programs. If your products or services require training client personnel, a boilerplate description of your training program could save time when you write the proposal. This file would include an explanation of your training approach, setup of classes, presentation of material, and expected results.

- Client references. RFPs usually require three or more client references attesting to the quality of your firm's work and overall performance. The information provided in these references generally includes a brief history of the client firm, the reason your company was chosen for the job, what product or service you provided that is still in place, and the title, name, and phone number and/or address of a direct contact in the client firm.

Time/Cost Section

Particularly in today's business environment, time/cost strategies must be factored into the proposal process from the beginning. Gone are the good old days when firms could assume that the client would pay whatever it took to get the best solution to the problem. You can be sure that the client's financial director will be scrutinizing every proposal for unrealistic estimates, hidden costs, and padded figures. With current operating and profit margins so thin, clients may put cost above other considerations when deciding between two similar proposals. In such cases, focusing on value-added services may be the best approach when writing the proposal. Clients may select a less-sophisticated product or service simply because they can afford it. Or they may ask for the bidders to resubmit their bids based on a lower cost strategy.

For many of today's clients, your time/cost strategy must accomplish three objectives:

1. *Demonstrate that you have an understanding of the client's financial situation.* Does the client have a fixed budget? a company estimate? Other resources from which to draw if needed? Your strategy should reflect your background research of the client's resources and show an appreciation for the client's circumstances.

2. *Cover the actual costs of the project.* This includes creating a final product or service, plus other services your firm may provide, such as implementing and monitoring. These cost estimates can be based on historical data of similar past projects (adjusted for inflation), additional outside staff who may be needed, equipment required, and so forth.

3. *Earn a profit for your firm.* Although this may seem too obvious to mention, it is surprising how many companies either break even or actually lose money on the projects they win. Remember, each proposal must support your company's own long-term strategy. To do so, you must have a realistic idea of what you need to charge in order to earn a profit on every job and what your profit margin needs to be. The profit margin may change from one job to the next.

These three objectives will help you avoid the temptation to cut costs or corners simply to submit a low bid. The right strategy can help you win the more lucrative contracts. Those who believe that the best cost strategy is "lower, lower, lower" may win their share of contracts, but they will miss out on many of the higher-paying jobs. There are three reasons why this is the case.

First, the client may have allocated funds to spend before a stated deadline. Although less common than in the past, this situation makes the client more concerned about spending the funds than saving money, out of fear that future allocations will be set at a lower level. As long as your proposal costs appear reasonable to the client, money will not be the deciding factor.

A second common situation in which the lowest bid might not win the contract occurs when the client has a fixed budget for the project.

In this case, the main concern will be getting the most value for their money. The client will be looking primarily for high-quality solutions at a cost within an established budget.

Finally, if your cost estimate is too far below your competitors' estimates, the client may feel that you cannot deliver a quality product or that you do not really understand the problem in the RFP. Either way, your proposal loses.

Having said this, however, we do not mean to suggest that you shouldn't try to find ways to lower costs where feasible. How and when you decide to do so depends on each individual project. For example, if you lower your bottom-line costs for an RFP, the additional funds can be used to add enhancements to the product or service that may make your proposal more attractive to the client.

You can lower your costs in several ways. One of the most effective is by designing an innovative system, product, or service that produces actual cost savings that can be passed on to the client. If this approach is not possible, you can attempt to minimize overhead costs as you work, which will result in a lower overhead rate and lower total costs to the client. If the RFP requires a labor-intensive product or service as a solution, the company with the lowest overhead rate usually wins the contract. Finally, consider other ways to reduce costs, such as subcontracting, forming joint teaming agreements, and other creative methods of getting the job done while maintaining quality.

Cost Categories. There are four broad cost categories that you need to address when developing cost estimates for your proposal: direct costs, overhead, general and administrative costs, and profit/fee.

Direct costs are those that can be charged to a specific contract. Examples of direct costs include employee compensation, materials and supplies, travel, telephone expenses, and printing.

Overhead costs are those costs associated with running your business that cannot be charged to a particular project. These expenses, such as utilities, rent, benefits, and salaries, must be absorbed by all the projects that your company takes on throughout the year.

General and Administrative (G&A) costs include marketing, legal fees, research and development, and general corporate expenses.

Finally, when developing cost estimates for any proposal, you will need to consider your firm's profit/fee. Your fee is comprised of the cost to your firm of the project plus a certain percentage over costs. Your profit is the fee less all costs associated with the project. You must be able to forecast your firm's expenses in the three areas above to calculate your profit/fee percentage for the RFP. For example, most contractors have a fixed percentage as a profit rate on material and a fixed dollar rate for profit on labor.

Note that your profit margin should be built into your costs. It should *not* be determined ahead of time, then allocated equally to each section of the project. You can easily price yourself out of a contract with this method. For example, some RFPs will state explicitly that general and administrative expenses cannot exceed 15 percent of the total cost of the bid. Some projects will require higher profit margins than others because they may be more labor-intensive or more difficult to perform.

Cost Strategies. Although there are several techniques for estimating costs, two of the more commonly used methods are the bottom-up approach and the top-down approach. The bottom-up approach is widely used for projects where costs are not the main concern. In this technique, the cost for each of the steps in the program design are determined and added to obtain a total cost.

The top-down technique is used more often when the project is cost-sensitive, if you have a good idea of the client's budget for the project, or if you know what your competitors are likely to bid. Using the top-down approach, you target a final cost estimate before beginning the project design. A percentage of this target cost is assigned to each task for the final project.

Whether you use the bottom-up or top-down approach, carefully review the dollar amounts and/or percentages in your estimate to be sure that you cover all costs and that they are reasonable for the RFP.

Some firms find it useful to develop a pro forma income statement that details all costs of a project. This method though more time-consuming, will provide you with more accurate cost estimates. If you are able to determine what the client is willing to expend on the project, your estimated dollar profit and return on investment can easily be calculated. This method also helps you determine whether your final profit or loss from the project is worth your time and effort.

As an alternative to preparing a pro forma income statement, you could prepare your cost statement or cost budget by major expense categories. These are the figures you would generally include in your proposal; detailed pro forma income statements are usually used for in-house analysis.

Even though the cost statement or budget is listed by major expense categories, it is strongly recommended that you perform a detailed cost analysis so you do not miss any cost categories. A shortened list of cost categories is shown in Exhibit 5.2.

Once you have completed a budget for the proposal, use variance analysis to keep track of cost overruns or underruns. This approach allows your firm's management to take corrective action immediately on any problems that arise to prevent them from becoming major crises.

Exhibit 5.2   Cost Budget—Direct Services

Project: _**BioCom**_

Project Manager: _**Carla Reiner**_

Category	Cost
Personnel - compensation	$ 42,000
Fringe benefits	12,500
Rental equipment cost	8,940
Lease Cost	6,723
Contract services	4,000
Building space	3,210
Supplies	5,306
Depreciation, taxes, insurance	2,587
Training expenses	9,500
Education expenses	860
Office expenses	7,500
Telephone	2,433
Travel	10,752
General & Administrative	8,900
% of overhead to apply ($)	10,016
Follow-up expenses	15,000
TOTAL COSTS	$150,227

It should be noted that the client can request a detailed breakdown of any category listed in a cost estimate. The client may want to see how you arrived at a figure. For example, you may list rental expenses for a 12-month project as $2,880. The client wants the total broken down by rental item:

Rental Expense: $2,880

Test equipment	–	$120/mo.	=	$1,440
Copier	–	$100/mo.	=	1,200
Fax machine	–	$20/mo.	=	240

If you have trouble developing a cost estimate for a particular project or cannot find sufficient information on the client's probable budget, you may want to consider developing your response to the RFP in stages instead of submitting a single response to the bid. For instance, in the first stage you would bid for doing the job well but with no extras or add-ons. This would cover only the baseline product or service needed to meet the RFP requirements. The second stage would involve a bid that included the most appropriate and attractive add-ons you believe the client would want. The final stage would be a bid for a "top-of-the-line" job with all the features and add-ons for maximum value (similar to a rate sheet).

Each of these stages is priced out separately, but developed in a modular format. Each stage can be performed quickly and easily without rebuilding the prior stages. This strategy presents the client with more possibilities than would a single response and offers them a wider range of choices. The client can take advantage of the schedule and contract for the job in phases as the money comes in.

If your cost estimates come in consistently high and are too far above the acceptable range for the bid, you will need to find ways of reducing your costs. Ways to do this include staging your proposal as described above, using innovative systems or approaches that lower your costs, finding ways to lower your overhead expenses, and, if all else fails, discounting. You can use new-account discounts, straight discounts, large-quantity discounts, and the like. However, one of the major drawbacks of this method is that clients may come to expect discounts in the future as well. You will have to make up your profit from other jobs, which may force you to price other RFPs higher than you ordinarily would.

If you cannot trim your costs to fit the contract range, consider walking away from the job. If winning a bid is going to have a negative impact on your firm, you may be better off turning the project down. Remember, your primary objective is to support your company's long-term marketing strategy and mission.

Time Strategy. Time strategies are based on your firm's prior experience with similar work and/or on careful research of similar types of projects. In some cases, such as software development, precise time estimates may be difficult to make. However, you should be able to establish some type of realistic schedule for the project. You may want to cite similar projects in a footnote or list them in a table to justify to the client why you have confidence in your time estimates.

A more sophisticated method for time estimation and reduction used by many firms is a technique called PERT/CPM (Program Evaluation and Review Technique with the Critical Path Method). This method identifies key tasks and subordinate tasks and organizes a time schedule so that key tasks are accomplished first. A discussion of PERT/CPM is beyond the scope of this book, but there are many operations research books that describe this method in detail.

The format for project schedules can vary from a simple timeline graph to more elaborate graphics. We recommend you keep the format clear and simple. For example:

Schedule for Software Development: October 14–December 17

Design and Program Development	October 14–November 3
Program Testing and Debugging	November 4–November 24
Field Testing/Refinement	November 25–December 17

The more technically difficult or abstract the project (e.g., improving worker efficiency and motivation), the longer the solution may take. Solutions to more concrete projects, such as redesigning work flow or developing a new distribution network, generally take less time to develop.

Who Reads the Time/Cost Section? In general, the accounting or finance group evaluates this section, although eventually everyone on the RFP committee or group will look it over. Time and cost evaluation in large companies is usually a formal process overseen by a member of senior management. The group will compare your cost estimates and time schedules with your competitors' and against the client's own experience with similar projects.

Your background research should determine whether the client has a formal or informal time/cost evaluation process, and the level of sophistication of the people who will be doing the analysis. This information can help you decide how much information to include and how you should organize and present the time and cost data.

For example, when the client has a more formal time/cost evaluation process, you would break down the schedule and cost estimate into more detail, providing justifications for each item. For a more informal process, you might emphasize broader time and cost categories, focusing on key schedule dates and the costs associated with each date. In this case, the client is not as interested in how you arrived at the figures as in what the figures cover and when you estimate payments will be made to your firm.

What Should It Look Like? The pricing section may be as simple as a list of equipment or services with the prices included, or it may be more detailed and include your cost estimating techniques. In many instances, your prices may be taken from standard price guides and be subject to little variation.

Bidding on state or federal contracts (e.g., for the Department of Defense) is a world all its own, and pricing is often based on the General Services Administration price list. Because government bids are complex to prepare, companies generally have a specialist on staff or hire consultants to put together the time/cost section for their proposals.

Your time/cost section usually contains the following information:

- Schedule of the work, generally with key completion dates for each stage—tells the client what will be done and when. Breaking the project down into stages gives the client a better idea of the time, staff, and resources required to complete each stage successfully.

- Cost summary—summarizes all costs for such categories as equipment; licensing fees; hardware and software; maintenance; project management; training; and implementation, administration, testing, and monitoring; and lists any discounts available.

- Cost totals—presents the bottom line total costs of the project
- Shipping and payment schedules—lists the equipment or services that will be delivered to the client and a payment schedule for work done and/or equipment or services delivered
- Standard terms and conditions—lets the client know under what conditions payment should be made and what is expected of both parties should there be delays or problems with the project. This part is, in effect, a contract for services between you and the client. Your firm may have a boilerplate agreement that can be inserted in each proposal. The terms can be changed during negotiations.

Separate Cost Volume. In some instances, you may wish to create a separate volume containing cost estimates and pricing. This may be particularly wise when you wish the client to evaluate the technical and management sections without being influenced by the cost. Generally, you make only one copy, marked CONFIDENTIAL and PROPRI-ETARY, and give it to top management or to the senior accounting or finance officer.

In rare instances, the cost volume may be submitted after the technical and management sections of the proposal have been evaluated. This may be true when cost estimates for a large proposal cannot be completed by the RFP due date because equipment prices and other cost data may not be available in time or may change rapidly. If you need more time to develop the cost section, discuss this with the client. It is always best to keep the client informed about your progress. No one likes unpleasant surprises.

The time/cost section of the proposal can be the most difficult section to develop. Not only are issues of scheduling and pricing hotly debated among the proposal team members, but the section is generally developed when the team is near exhaustion. As a result, this section often requires more time and effort than expected at the outset of the proposal-writing process.

Make sure that your are well-prepared by gathering pricing information early in the process and by making changes as the proposal is developed. Also, keep management interference to a minimum. Pricing is one area that will unfailingly attract upper management's attention. They may want to review the figures or help to develop the section without having sufficient information about the scope and program design of the proposal. Being concerned with the bottom line, they may criticize the cost estimates or suggest cuts or additions that are not in line with the rest of the proposal.

Lastly, the client may request changes that will affect your time/cost estimates. For example, the client may want to add or subtract tasks to the original RFP that will reduce or extend the timeline for the project. These changes may also force you to subtract or add staff to the project.

In another instance, a client may want to add or subtract equipment, services, or processes; reduce or increase the scope of the project; or make unexpected requests that will force you to restructure the entire time/cost section. Keep in mind that if the job is one you definitely want, you may be able to outlast your competition by responding with timely, professional answers to the client's requests.

ABOUT APPENDICES

Appendices contain supplemental material that can be used to support or illustrate your technical, management, or time/cost sections or simply provide additional information to the client. Appendices are named by letters, not numbers: Appendix A, Appendix B, etc.

Material included in the appendices is generally too detailed to put into the main body of the proposal. A complete list of equipment and parts pricing, for example, is suitable for an appendix but may be too long and detailed for the cost section of the proposal. In the text, you point out where this additional material can be found: "For a complete list of equipment prices, see Appendix A." Each appendix is referenced in the appropriate section of the proposal. If you add or subtract appendices, be sure that references to these appendices in the proposal text are also added or deleted. It can be embarrassing for a client to ask "Where is Appendix C?" when you have eliminated it from the proposal.

The appendices should contain only material that is directly related to the proposal. Resist the temptation to include information that is nice to know but not essential for the client to have. Also, make sure you have put all important data in the text. Do not depend on appendix material to fulfill an RFP requirement.

Some information generally included in appendices includes:

- Industry surveys, reports, and statistics
- Company brochures and other data
- Sample contracts and letters of agreement
- Sample training class syllabi and schedules
- Policies and guidelines
- Reprints of relevant articles or technical data sheets
- Annual reports and financial data

SUMMARY OF A WINNING PROGRAM DESIGN

As we've seen in this chapter, program design is the heart of your proposal. Your winning program design must do the following:

- Convince the client that you understand the client's problems even better than the client does and that you have a unique selling point to solve those problems.
- Present a concise, detailed plan for solving those problems within the requirements of the RFP. The plan and all detail strategies should emphasize your strengths to the client.
- Provide technical, management, and time/cost strategies that tell the client what will be done, how it will be done, who will do it, how long it will take, and how much it will cost.
- Convince the client that you will absolutely be able to implement the program design. If you or your client have any doubts about this, you should think twice about submitting your proposal.
- Above all, your program design should sell the client on your firm and not just on your product or service ideas.

CHAPTER
≡ SIX

WRITING THE FRONT MATTER AND EXECUTIVE SUMMARY

The proposal team was approaching the final stages of development. The program design had been approved by top management, and the vice president had given Ms. Reiner a list of key points to include in the executive summary.

"You've all done a great job so far," Ms. Reiner told the proposal team. "I know it has been an exhausting process, but we're almost there. We've got one more critical part to develop: the Executive Summary."

Masters asked, "What about the cover letter and the table of contents?"

"The writing team is covering those. But you and Ed know the program design inside and out. I want you two to come up with a rough draft of the Executive Summary. The writers will polish it after you get through."

She handed the two researchers a copy of the key elements list for the summary.

"Management wants these points emphasized. We have a great chance at winning this bid, so sell the client hard on our design and experience. Hook them on our value-added features and get them to believe we're the only ones who can do this project for them."

"All of that in two pages?" Breen asked.

"Go to three if you have to, but keep it short and to the point."

Masters looked over the key elements list. "Give us a couple of days and we'll see what we come up with."

"Remember," Ms. Reiner said, "You're not just explaining our program—you're doing a sales job. So grab the client's attention and don't let go!"

• • •

STEP 7: FRONT MATTER AND EXECUTIVE SUMMARY

Once you have written the program design and a draft of the proposal, it will be reviewed and revised by upper management. When the final content is approved, you will need to develop the front matter and executive summary to complete the proposal. The front matter includes the cover letter (also known as the letter of transmittal), title page, proprietary notice, table of contents, and list of illustrations.

The executive summary presents the main highlights of your proposal and gives you an opportunity to sell your solution and your company to the client. It is generally only one to two pages in length, although multi-volume proposals may have longer executive summaries. In this chapter, we provide guidelines for creating these materials and present samples illustrating each one. A sample executive summary is provided in Appendix A.

THE FRONT MATTER

Cover (Transmittal) Letter

A well-thought-out cover letter can motivate the client to take a closer look at your proposal. It is usually bound into the proposal so that it is not accidentally lost or separated from the proposal itself. It should be signed by the senior officer on the project or the president or CEO of your firm. The cover letter is less formal in tone than either the executive summary or the proposal, and is considered a commitment from your senior executives to the client's officers. (See Exhibit 6.1 for a sample cover letter.) Cover letters are a page or two in length and consist of at least three paragraphs.

The opening paragraph provides a brief statement or summary of your marketing strategy or theme. Avoid the simple "thank you for allowing us to bid" statement. You need a stronger opening that emphasizes your product or service and why the client should choose your company over all the others.

The middle paragraph(s) offers a brief statement of the unique selling point that will meet and exceed the client's needs. This is an opportunity to capture the client's interest and imagination in ways that go beyond the RFP.

Exhibit 6.1   Sample Cover Letter

Company Letterhead and Logo

October 30, 19—

Dr. H. M. Vencore, President
BioCom Medicare Services, Inc.
313 North Riverside Drive
Chicago, IL 60603

Dear Dr. Vencore:

Andover Medical Consultants is proposing a complete solution for BioCom's Medical Format Software (MFS) Program. Andover and our associate firm, Software Tracks, Inc., have the combined resources to ensure that the software requirements in the RFP are fully realized with a powerful, versatile program that meets and exceeds all technical specifications found in BioCom's documentation. We also have developed a strategic marketing plan for the MFS Program that will enable BioCom to gain a significant share of the medical software market even in the face of rapid advances in computer technology.

Andover offers a two-tiered solution to BioCom's needs. Phase I involves the development of a MFS Program that provides unique functions in data reporting, statistical manipulation, and correlation of key elements. Phase II is a complete marketing plan for the software that includes sales force training and field demonstrations. Andover will fully support both the software and the marketing plan after the project is completed.

Because Andover has had extensive experience in developing medical software, we feel that BioCom's 18-month schedule is not only possible but comfortable. We have a file of successful programs to serve as the foundation for the new software. Due to the highly technical nature of this proposal, we would welcome the opportunity to make a personal presentation to your management staff. This would enable your staff and ours to clarify any points before the final proposal evaluation.

Andover's proposal for the Medical Format Software Program (#3755) and pricing are valid for 60 days. Mr. Arnis Tadeski, an officer of Andover, is authorized to make all commitments presented in this proposal. Please direct all future communications to Ms. Carla Reiner, who is managing the proposal process. Please include our proposal number in all future communications.

We look forward to working with you on the Medical Format Software Program.

Sincerely yours,

Arnis Tadeski

President

Carla Reiner

Vice President, Operations

Also, use these middle paragraphs to explain any special research or other efforts you took to identify critical requirements in the RFP, or additional client needs you spotted that may have been implied but not explicitly stated in the RFP.

The closing paragraph usually includes references to the RFP number (if one is given) and project name; length of time the proposal is valid; a statement verifying that the signer of the letter is authorized by your firm; and the name and address of the person in your firm who will act as the contact for future correspondence from the client. *Do not allow any other person in your company to talk with the client.* This policy prevents any confusion, mixed messages, or miscommunications between your firm and the client.

Title Page

The title page format will vary according to each company—many firms have a company style for their proposal covers. Exhibit 6.2 shows a sample of one firm's title page. In general, the page will contain the following:

- *Response to Requirements* printed above the project name.
- The client's name and address and the name of the person who signed the RFP. Check with the client to verify where, to whom, and how to submit the proposal.
- *Submitted by* line printed above your firm's name, logo, and address.
- Proposal number—refer to this number in your cover letter and request that the client refer to it in any correspondence. This adds a professional touch to your work and identifies each proposal in your data banks.
- In highly sensitive proposals, you may wish to assign a *controlled document number.* That is, if you distribute five copies, each copy will have an assigned number (one through five) in addition to the proposal number. A controlled document number allows you to keep track of each proposal. The number can be printed in red on the original copies. In this way, if anyone makes an unauthorized reproduction, the number will photocopy in black. It will be easy to spot a pirated copy of the proposal.

- *Date*—this must be the date the proposal is due, *not* the date you submit the proposal.

In some cases, you may want to designate one copy of the proposal as the *Master Copy.* This one will contain the original cover letter, while the others will have copies of the cover letter. If you designate a master copy, be sure to print MASTER COPY on the proposal cover and title page.

Exhibit 6.2   Sample Title Page

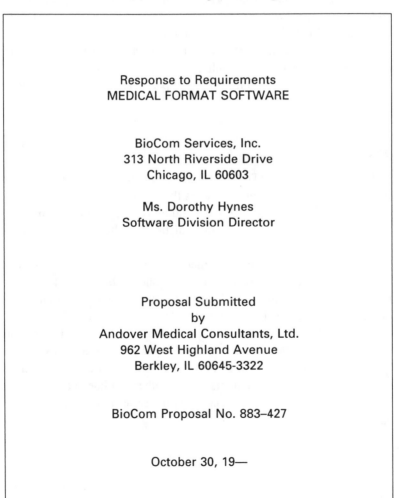

Response to Requirements
MEDICAL FORMAT SOFTWARE

BioCom Services, Inc.
313 North Riverside Drive
Chicago, IL 60603

Ms. Dorothy Hynes
Software Division Director

Proposal Submitted
by
Andover Medical Consultants, Ltd.
962 West Highland Avenue
Berkley, IL 60645-3322

BioCom Proposal No. 883–427

October 30, 19—

Proprietary Notice

Although not all proposals require a proprietary notice, it's a good rule of thumb to include it in any proposal you submit. The notice should appear on the bottom of each page, unless you have a nondisclosure statement. Basically, the notice states that the information contained in your proposal should not be released to anyone outside those who will evaluate it for the client. You need to protect your information from competitors and others who may use it without your permission and without giving you credit.

Remember, if you do not protect your work with the proprietary notice, your competitors can ask for and receive copies of your proposal under the federal Freedom of Information Act.

Because the requirements of each firm vary, there is no generic proprietary notice form. Consult your legal department or a lawyer familiar with this area to help you draw up a notice that meets the needs of your company.

Table of Contents

The table of contents (TOC) is a list of all the major sections and subsections in your proposal. It helps the client find specific information quickly. TOCs vary widely depending on the length, complexity, and number of volumes of your proposal, but the following general rules apply to nearly all TOCs.

First, use either a Roman numeral or numbered format for your headings (see Exhibit 6.3). If you have a short table of contents, you may want to list only the major headings. For a longer proposal, list only the first two levels of headings in the TOC.

Second, if you have more than one volume, include the TOCs from all the volumes in the first one (see Exhibit 6.4). Subsequent volumes generally list only their own contents. However, you may prefer to include a brief table of contents for the other volumes as well. This approach may help the client keep the entire series in mind as they read each volume.

Exhibit 6.3   Sample Tables of Contents—Single-Volume Proposal

A. Full Table of Contents

TABLE OF CONTENTS

B. Short Table of Contents

TABLE OF CONTENTS

Exhibit 6.4 Sample Table of Contents—Multiple-Volume Proposal

Volume 1: Technical Section
TABLE OF CONTENTS

Volume 2: Management Approach
TABLE OF CONTENTS

Volume 3: Time/Cost Estimates
Table of Contents

List of Illustrations and Tables

The lists of illustrations and tables follow the TOC, and should be printed on separate pages, unless they are very short, in which case they can appear on a single page (see Exhibit 6.5).

Exhibit 6.5   Sample List of Illustrations and List of Tables

Illustrations

LIST OF ILLUSTRATIONS

Page

Tables

LIST OF TABLES

Additional Front Matter

In addition to these items, there might be additional material you want
to add to the front matter of your proposal. Common additions include
a list of abbreviations, a compliance matrix and exceptions list, and an
explanatory preface if your proposal is particularly complex.

Abbreviations List. You may want to include an abbreviations list as
a key to the trade names, acronyms, and buzz words unique to your
company or business. Such a list is generally part of your boilerplate
files and is placed after the lists of illustrations or tables in your
proposal.

Compliance Matrix and Exceptions List. Many government RFPs
require a compliance matrix to show that you have met the major
requirements and specifications in the RFP. If you cannot be compliant
in all areas, you should explain each exception. For example, you may
have a product or service that makes one or two requirements unnec-
essary. By explaining your reasons, you have a chance to highlight
certain features of your product or service.

"How to Read This Proposal." If your proposal is complex and difficult to follow, you may want to provide a preface to help readers find their way through the text.

In addition to these features, some RFPs may require you to establish a bond (bid check, performance bond, payment bond) when you submit the proposal. Others may require you to sign a "Buy USA Statement" in which you agree that a certain percentage of any equipment you buy will be manufactured in the United States.

THE EXECUTIVE SUMMARY

The executive summary is far more than a one- or two-page summary or abstract of what is presented in your proposal. (See Appendix A for a sample Executive Summary.) In addition to providing the main points of the individual sections, you can use the summary to:

- demonstrate your grasp of the client's problem
- sell your solution and its benefits over your competitors' solutions and benefits
- educate the client about your firm and its products, staff, and resources
- explain your program design and its outstanding features and benefits in more detail
- translate complex technical concepts, products, or processes into readily understandable terms
- present pertinent information not requested in the RFP
- reinforce how the client will benefit by having your firm do the job

The executive summary is your most effective and important selling piece and deserves all the effort and attention you can give it. Remember, the client may receive dozens of proposals and may use the executive summary as an initial screening process. The primary focus of the executive summary is on what results can be achieved by your product or service. How those results will be achieved is less important here—for those details, the client must read the proposal.

Who Reads the Executive Summary?

Although the executive summary is read by a wide range of people in the client's organization, your main audience is the top executive or executive group with the authority to award the job. This person or group reads all of the executive summaries in order to grasp the major strengths, weaknesses, and differences of each proposal. Your executive summary is an opportunity to sell this person or group on your solution and on your firm. Remember, the focus is on results and value for price rather than on how the results will be achieved.

The executive summary is also read by other members of the evaluation staff to gain an overview of your proposal before they examine its more detailed sections. In this way, the staff members have a context for judging your program design and will better understand your technical approach, management plan, and time/cost estimates. You are giving the evaluation staff the main features and benefits of your proposal from a business point of view and not from strictly a technical viewpoint. Whether you also include the pricing strategy in the executive summary is a matter of judgment. You will have to determine whether there is some advantage for doing so in each case.

The executive summary is designed to answer a progressive series of questions:

1. What is your solution?
2. Why was that solution chosen and how did you arrive at it?
3. What are the details of the solution (usually, the technical aspects)?
4. How will the project be managed?
5. What happens after the project is finished?
6. How much time and money will it require?
7. Who is your firm and why do you believe you can do the job?

Outline of the Executive Summary

Most RFPs provide little guidance for developing the executive summary. They may ask you to provide a brief description or outline of the proposed solution; avoid excessive technical detail or jargon, and include any areas of concern that need to be addressed. They may even state that no pricing or time/cost estimates should be included. However, you must still interpret what is meant by "brief description or outline" and "any areas of concern that need to be addressed."

In their RFP guidelines, companies ask bidders to examine their solutions for weaknesses and remedies and to show that they understand the client's problems and know how to address them. As a result, the executive summary should contain at least an introduction to the proposed solution, a brief description of that solution and its benefits to the client, and who is providing the solution. In general, executive summaries contain some or all of the following elements, which are discussed in more detail below:

- Introduction
- Program design
- Technical approach
- Project management plan
- Implementation, monitoring, maintenance
- Training
- Time/cost
- Company profile
- Future products or services

You may not need all of these items for every one of the executive summaries you write. For example, on some projects you may not be involved with implementation, monitoring, or maintenance, or you may not be required to train the client's workforce.

Introduction

By the time you are ready to write the executive summary, you should know the client and the client's problems so well that you can put yourself in the decision-maker's shoes and ask, "What would I want to know from this executive summary? What would grab my attention and keep me reading?

Would you want to wade through an extensive description of the bidder's company, how fantastic their products or services are, and their qualifications—or would you want to know what the bidder is going to do for you?

Opening Paragraphs

Your first few paragraphs must start off selling your solution. Many companies make the mistake of launching into a detailed profile of their firm and its capabilities, reciting a list of successful products or similar jobs that were completed satisfactorily. But the current client cares more about the immediate problems than about your past successes!

The first paragraphs must accomplish the following three goals:

1. Restate the client's primary problem or goal and set the tone for the proposal.
2. Present your firm's solution or promise to meet the goal.
3. Establish the proposal theme, which is reinforced throughout each section.

Remember, positive selling is far more powerful and effective than negative selling. Tell the client what they can gain by awarding you the job—not what they'll lose if they don't hire you.

The example paragraphs below illustrate a winning proposal opening.

BioCom's goal of facilitating communications among innovative drug treatment programs requires a sophisticated medical software program that goes beyond the usual management information system. As stated in the RFP, this software must be compatible with a variety of hardware systems; convert data from various formats into one uniform format; and be flexible, easily upgraded, and user-friendly. In addition to the RFP requirements, we also see the need for BioCom to develop a marketing and sales strategy for the software to position the company in the forefront of this market by offering superior service to its software customers.

Our solution will provide BioCom not only with the software program it needs but also with an effective marketing and sales strategy to make the most of the opportunities the software presents. The strategy will position BioCom for future growth and enable the company to respond quickly to technological changes in computer hardware and software.

It is our intention in this proposal to describe how we will accomplish these goals and to demonstrate our firm's commitment to assist BioCom in achieving its corporate objectives for growth and customer service.

These opening paragraphs draw the client into the proposal and promise a solution that other bidders, it is hoped, will be unable to match or surpass. The paragraphs also point out a new requirement that the original RFP did not contain but that may be critical to the client's success and future growth. Right away, the reader is hooked and eager to turn the page to find out more.

Program Design

While the introduction announces the solution to the client's problem, this section of the executive summary states briefly how and why you developed this particular solution. You are answering the question "Why did we choose this solution, and how did we develop it?"

In this section, you need to show that you understand not only what is requested in the RFP but also the problems associated with finding the right solution. You can present your case in terms of trade-offs, that is, the benefits and costs of each option. This section should show the client why your solution offers the best cost/benefit ratio.

For example, BioCom's software program may provide greater flexibility but also require large amounts of computer memory to run the program. However, since many small computers now have the memory capacity of a mainframe computer, this cost can be relatively insignificant to the client. The bidder could explain that reducing the flexibility of the program simply to free up more computer memory would be a poor trade-off.

Technical Approach

The technical approach section of the executive summary answers the question "What are the details of the solution?" After reading this part, the client should have a good grasp of the main features of the solution and be able to determine if they meet the requirements of the RFP.

Keep in mind that you are writing this part for a largely nontechnical audience. Top management decision-makers may not have the expertise to understand the precise technical aspects of the product or service proposed. For example, BioCom executives may not be able to follow a discussion of the logic architecture of the software program, but they would understand a description of its features and how it would enable them to achieve their goals.

Make sure you explain key terms and keep all technical jargon and details to a minimum. If the client needs more information, you can designate one person on your staff to answer their questions or refer the client to the appropriate appendix in the proposal. Your main focus is to emphasize how the solution is tailor-made for the client's needs.

Project Management Plan

The more complex or technical the project, the more important a solid management plan becomes. Like the technical approach portion, this part of the executive summary should be a brief description of the management plan. In this section, you need to answer the following questions:

- How will the project be managed?
- Who will be on the project team?
- What responsibilities will each member assume?
- What will the proposed schedule be?
- How will your firm and client personnel interact?

You can include a brief work schedule and go into slightly more detail in the time/cost portion. Or, if the RFP states that no cost information should be included, you can present your work schedule plan in greater detail here. Be sure to state clearly management's role in each step of the work schedule—that is, indicate who will be supervising which tasks of the project. If you will be using a joint consultant/ client management team, clarify which responsibilities will be delegated to which personnel and who will be the contact person for both parties.

Implementation, Monitoring, and Maintenance

Today, the demand for quality implementation, monitoring, and maintenance services is increasing. This trend is occurring for several reasons. First, clients must determine their return on investment based not only on initial costs but on implementation and maintenance expenses as well. If the initial price is a bargain but the cost of maintaining a product or service over time is high, the clients haven't received the best value for their money.

Implementation, monitoring, and maintenance are also critical when companies win jobs in areas where they do not have adequately trained maintenance personnel, when they bid products that have not been fully tested, or when they are caught short of staff and funding due to rapid growth, merger or acquisition.

Finally, client service and support is an important way of distinguishing yourself from the competition and offering more value for the client's money.

Many clients, to protect themselves, include penalty clauses if their new system is down for more than a specified amount of time or if client personnel find the new product, service, or process too difficult, cumbersome, or inefficient to use. In most cases, bidders cannot issue a warranty on many of the services they provide to clients. As a result, a quality implementation, monitoring, and maintenance plan can ensure the client's satisfaction with your work after the initial project is completed.

When writing this section, you are answering the question "What happens after the project is finished?" The client will want to know how you will help to introduce the product or service to their firm and how you will support your work once the final payment has been made. Remember: *strong customer service can be the value-added feature that helps you stand out from the competition.* In many instances, this feature carries greater weight than the cost component when a client is making a final decision.

Training

The client must also be confident that your firm can provide the training needed to make workers skilled in the use of new software, equipment, or procedures or processes you develop. This section of the summary should serve as a brief overview of your training department or function and should include basic information on the following subjects:

- Your training staff and their qualifications
- Types of instruction you use (computer-assisted, interactive video, lecture, self-learning)
- Provisions for training at your facility or on site at the client's location

- Follow-up training for those who require it (new employees, transferred staff, etc.)

If you present a comprehensive, well-written overview of your training capabilities, you send a message to the reader that your company knows what it takes to develop a successful solution. You also appear to be a well-organized and established firm capable of backing up your work.

Time/Cost

The time/cost section in the executive summary is generally an optional feature, but it can make a strong argument for your firm and can be one of the most persuasive sections in the executive summary. Some RFPs specifically request that pricing be omitted because it may influence a selection that should be based on program design or some other feature.

If the RFP you are responding to does not explicitly exclude pricing information, you have a good opportunity to sell your firm in this part. You can provide a summary of your schedule and costs and explain briefly any special conditions, exceptions, additions, or discounts that were involved in developing the final estimates. You can also use the pricing summary to mention any special terms and conditions in the RFP, explain any optional products or services not requested in the RFP, and justify any exceptions to RFP requirements. You should also use this section to highlight any price/value advantages you may have over your competition (special supplier arrangements, shipping discounts, proprietary information, software licenses, etc.).

The time/cost section also offers you an opportunity to present alternative schedules and cost structures. You may have developed two or three time/cost estimates based on what the client wants done and how quickly it needs to be accomplished. Some clients may award more evaluation points to firms that offer the fastest installation time.

You can also explain any deviations from the RFP—for example, why you are not bidding on a portion of the RFP or what additions to the RFP requirements you believe are necessary. For instance, you may see a need to add equipment or staff to the project that the client did not anticipate.

Even if your estimated costs are higher than those of your competitors, your firm won't automatically be eliminated from the bidding—

provided you can justify those costs. The price/value trade-off has to make sense to the client in order for you to sell your solution.

Corporate Profile

The corporate profile gives you an opportunity to introduce your company and highlight its unique resources and capabilities. If the client has worked with your firm previously, this part of the summary gives you an opportunity to update the client on your firm's current resources and strengths. This can be particularly important if your firm has grown considerably or changed its focus in the past few years. The client may remember a much smaller, more limited firm or a company in another line of business.

Your corporate profile should include at least the following information:

- When the company was founded and a statement of its mission or objective
- A brief history of the company's development and contributions to the industry
- Types of equipment/products/services you provide
- Company organization and the features and benefits thereof
- Locations of headquarters and divisions or affiliates, and number of employees

It is often useful to include an organizational chart of departments or divisions and top management (president/CEO, vice presidents, executive directors, etc.) and a map showing your firm's locations and affiliates. These graphics enable the reader to grasp your company's organization and size at a glance.

After reading this section, the client should have a solid understanding of who and what your firm is and where the client's project will be placed in your organization.

Future Products and Other Elements

Like the time/cost section, this part of the executive summary is optional and gives you the chance to comment on current or late-breaking technology or other events related to the client's problems and opportunities. If appropriate, you may wish to include a final section outlining what you believe to be future spinoffs or directions the company could take based on the current proposed project. Or you may wish to share information on where future technology is going to show the client they are buying into a product, service, or process that will help them stay abreast or even ahead of their changing markets. For example, you may know of a recent breakthrough in genetic engineering or material science that may indicate potential new resources or markets for the client in the near future.

This part can demonstrate your company's ability to keep pace with current changes in technology, marketing, and resources. The message you give the client is that your firm has financial and human resource strengths that may not be obvious in other parts of your proposal.

COMMON ERRORS

Look over the following list of common errors that companies make in writing the executive summary. Check your past proposals or your rough draft of the summary to make sure you have not made these common mistakes.

- Forgetting who the primary audience is—the primary decision makers (top management) generally read the executive summary; some may read *only* the summary and leave the rest of the proposal to the technical managers.
- Writing an opening paragraph that is too general and/or too negative—fear tactics are not good selling tools.
- Going into too much detail regarding *how* results will be achieved—remember, the client firm is interested primarily in the general solution to its problems and not the details about every step in the process.
- Including material that the RFP has expressly stated should *not* be included (e.g., scheduling or pricing information).
- Using too many technical terms or jargon—readers of the executive summary often are not experts in the technical aspects of your solution.

- Using too many graphics or additional materials—keep it simple; use only the graphics that are absolutely necessary to clarify your text (e.g., organization charts, flow charts).

Executive Summary Checklist

☐ Did you examine the RFP carefully to determine what should or should not be included in the executive summary?

☐ Do you know the client's level of knowledge and expertise?

☐ Is the summary focused on results, not details?

☐ Do your opening paragraphs focus on the client's problems and your solution and establish the proposal theme?

☐ In the program design section, did you briefly explain how and why you developed your solution?

☐ Did you explain the technical aspects by emphasizing benefits and minimizing technical jargon and details?

☐ In presenting the project management plan, did you include the following?

  ☐ how the project will be managed

  ☐ who will be on the project team

  ☐ what are the responsibilities of each member

  ☐ what is the proposed work schedule

  ☐ how your firm and client will interact

☐ Did you emphasize customer service in your implementation, monitoring, and maintenance section?

☐ Did you include the following in your training section?

  ☐ brief overview of your training department

  ☐ training staff

  ☐ types of instruction you use

  ☐ description of in-house and client site training facilities

  ☐ follow-up training procedures

☐ If the time/cost section is included, did you:

  ☐ mention any special terms and conditions

- ☐ explain any optional products, equipment, services not requested in the RFP
- ☐ justify exceptions to the RFP
- ☐ highlight price-value advantages you have over your competition
- ☐ offer alternative time schedules and cost estimates
- ☐ Have you used the corporate profile to include at least the following:
  - ☐ company founding and primary mission
  - ☐ brief history of development and contributions to industry
  - ☐ equipment/products/services you offer
  - ☐ company organization and its features and benefits
  - ☐ number and location of facilities or affiliates and number of employees
- ☐ Did you mention any future products or other essential information?
- ☐ Did you keep graphics and illustrations to a minimum?

The executive summary is the part of your proposal that serves as your public relations and sales presentation. The time and effort you spend on this section can be an invaluable investment not only for the current job but for future business from the client as well.

CHAPTER
≡SEVEN

PRODUCING YOUR PROPOSAL

"Ed, can you give me a hand with this section?" Tracy asked.

Ed Breen wheeled his chair over to Masters' computer station and peered at the text on her screen.

"What's the problem?"

"I can't seem to get the sequence right for the marketing strategy. I have to tell the client how the strategy will look today and in three years."

"Why not show it in a graph?"

"I tried a line graph, but there are too many parameters."

"No, no. The company's got a graphics file for showing marketing strategy over time. Here, call up File MS.23. I used it last month for the Fournier strategic marketing study we did."

"Perfect! I'll just add in my figures. You saved me a day's work. I have to get this section finished for the production coordinator by tomorrow. Ms. Reiner wants us to present the final draft to the executive committee on Friday."

"I know. Paula over in Finance said they've got two teams working on the time and cost estimates to get them done on schedule."

Masters sat back, shaking her head. "Why is it that no matter how soon we start a proposal, the production stage is always like a marathon race?"

•   •   •

STEP 8: PROPOSAL PRODUCTION

Once you have all the sections of the proposal complete, you can begin the production stage to put together a complete proposal. The team manager may coordinate this effort, or may turn the proposal drafts over to a production supervisor to have the work done. Production usually occurs in the following order:

1. Rough drafts of all sections and graphics are given to the production team.

2. The final proposal design and production budget are developed and approved. (The production budget is generally part of the original budget for proposal development.)

3. A complete document is assembled and submitted to top management for review.

4. All changes are inserted into the document; it is given a final edit, proofread, and printed. (Depending on the proposal, steps 3 and 4 may be repeated several times before a final document is approved.)

5. Top management and all team members read the proposal in a final review.

6. Any further corrections are made.

7. The document is printed, bound, and delivered to top management and the client.

Because time is usually short by the time you reach this stage, planning is critical. All the various elements of the proposal—title page, table of contents and list of illustrations, cover letter, executive summary, body of the proposal, appendices, and any other supporting material—must be ushered through production to bound volume. Countless decisions must be made along the way: what type of binding should be used? Should the proposal be printed in black and white or color? What typeface should be used? How will last-minute changes be implemented? What if an illustration is added or deleted?

All these decisions, and the production tasks involved, can be made easier by having a production control schedule to keep track of each step in the process. Exhibit 7.1 shows an example of the production form similar to those used by many companies. The production coordinator can see at a glance what needs to be done, when it is due, and who has primary responsibility.

Production Guidelines

With today's computer hardware and software, even a small firm can produce high-quality, professional proposals at a reasonable cost. The real trick is not to get the fanciest software but to know how to use formatting, type styles, and graphics and illustrations to your best advantage. Buy the software and hardware systems that best meet your company's needs. The right presentation of your data can make it easier for the client to read, understand, and appreciate your grasp of their situation and your proposed solutions. If you do not already have desktop publishing capability, consult a computer specialist who can help you set up your system.

This chapter focuses on helping you learn the basics of producing a proposal, particularly using graphics and illustrations to give you the best chance at winning the contract. It is assumed that you have the software to develop your graphics in-house.

Exhibit 7.1 Proposal Production Schedule

RFP: Biocom												Date: 9/1–9/25	
Task	9/1	9/5	9/6	9/10	9/11	9/12	9/13	9/15	9/18	9/21	9/22	9/25	Responsibilities and Comments
First Draft													
• Executive Summary—Edit	X												W. Peters & C. Andes
• Cover Letter—Edit		X	X	X									C. Andes
• Proposal Chapters—Edit		X	X	X									Proposal Team
• Appendices—Edit					X								Proposal Team
• Illustrations					X								Graphics Department
Review First Draft						X							VP Carlos Lee
Final Draft													
• Executive Summary							X						Peters & Andes
• Cover Letter								X					Andes
• Proposal Chapters								X	X	X			Proposal Mgr. Ent
• Appendices									X	X			Proposal Team
• Illustrations									X				Graphics
Production													Production Department
• Binders											X		S. Ubland
Sign-Off											X		VP Carlos Lee
Delivery												X	Ent

Know Your Client

The rule "know your client" is as true for the production side of proposal writing as it is for the developmental side. Is the client known for being conservative, innovative, middle of the road? Examine client publications for clues to their preferences in production. Does the client use full-color displays in its publications? Or does the client seem attracted to more conservative displays and colors? Even if your firm has a standard format for creating a proposal, you can and should use your computer to customize the cover, add graphics and illustrations, and vary the type used in printing the document.

Get to know the "personality" or style of the client firm and tailor your production preparation accordingly. One firm jeopardized its proposal by opting for modernistic, abstract illustrations and covers. The client was a fairly conservative manufacturing company and had the impression that the proposal team didn't really understand the nature of the manufacturing business.

A clash between the proposal's style and the client's preferred style puts needless obstacles in your path. Take the time to do a little research on the client's expectations and preferences. This is not to say you shouldn't ever take chances by designing a more interesting cover or inserting a few artistic graphics. Just be sure that the client is likely to be pleasantly surprised by them and not left wondering for whom the proposal was designed.

Format—Swipe Files and Boilerplates

Most firms have an established format for their proposals. Proposal writers simply follow the format to create the title page, table of contents, executive summary, headings and divisions of each section, and appendices. Some firms may use a variety of formats, depending on the type of project for which they are bidding.

In many instances, writers do not have to create all the elements of a proposal. Items such as contracts, time/cost sections, company qualifications, list of work done for previous clients, and staff resumes can be placed in computer swipe files or as part of the company boilerplates. This information can then be called up from these files and inserted into the document at the appropriate places. Shortcuts like these make it easier to assemble a proposal, particularly when time is critical and the production schedule is short. Computer files can store a large variety of swipe files and boilerplate material, but the material must be updated periodically to be of any use.

GRAPHICS: How and Why to Use Them

Most people are familiar with tables, charts, and graphs—they are a common staple of business reports, newspapers, and even television news. But few people understand *why* particular data are shown using particular kinds of tables, charts, or graphs. In this section, we review the purpose of the most common graphic formats and which types of data are best displayed using each one.

Criteria for Using Graphics Instead of Words

In determining when to use words and when to use tables and other illustrations, keep the following criteria in mind as you are developing drafts of your proposal sections. Tables, charts, and graphs are better than words when:

- You need to describe complex technical or physical processes. How does cocaine affect the human body? How does an assembly line work? How will changes in an inner city design affect traffic flow in and around the area?

- You have complex numerical or statistical data to convey. You are summarizing the results of public opinion surveys on the client's new product offerings. Or you wish to present the results of drug rehabilitation treatment programs for 50 clinics. One table or chart can save you a page or two of text and present the data in a form the reader can grasp far more easily.

- You are describing something that requires the reader to form a mental image in order to understand it. A city plan, the interior of a building, the inner workings of a cell or virus—all these can be described verbally but are far clearer when presented in an illustration. A picture gives the reader a visual reference as your text continues.

- You want to present information in a form the reader will be able to recall easily. In general, most people remember visual

Exhibit 7.2   Visual Presentation of Text Information

Four Elements of Excellent Software

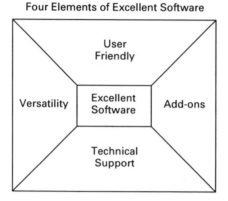

images better than they do words. If you are talking about the four critical elements of excellent software, for example, you might use a graph, such as the one shown in Exhibit 7.2, to present the information visually.

As you develop your draft proposal, note in the margins where you think tables, charts, or other graphics will be needed.

USING GRAPHICS AND ILLUSTRATIONS EFFECTIVELY

There are two principles governing the use of charts, tables, and other graphic materials:

1. *Illustrations should be essential to your proposal and not used to conceal a lack of content.* Illustrations must provide important information and not be used simply to fill out the page or to impress the client.

2. *Illustrations must support and clarify the text, not stand in place of it.* Illustrations must be properly labeled, inserted in the right place, and explained or interpreted in the text. You cannot assume the reader will understand what the illustration presents. The intricate structure of a robotics welding machine, for example, must have some type of accompanying caption or text explaining its salient features and drawbacks.

Types of Illustrations

There are six basic forms available to illustrate information in your proposal: tables, pie or circle graphs, bar charts, line graphs, organization and flow charts, and pictures or symbols. Exhibits 7.3 through 7.8 provide examples of all six types of illustrations. Which one you choose depends on the information you have to display and the point you are trying to make.

For example, suppose you are examining changes in the characteristics of drug users who enroll in drug treatment programs. You want to compare 1990 and 1995 data on this topic. The paragraph in your rough draft might read as follows:

> From 1990 to 1995, the characteristics of drug users enrolling in drug treatment programs changed considerably. In 1990, those aged 13 to 18 years comprised 42% of all enrollees, those aged 19 to 29 comprised 21%, those aged 30 to 45 comprised 15%, and those over 45 comprised 22%. In 1995, these figures had shifted dramatically. Enrollees 13 to 18 years of age represented only 35% of all enrollees, the 19 to 29 age group increased to 43%, the 30 to 45 age group accounted for only 12%, and the over-45 age group only represented 10% of the total.

This is a lot of data for the reader to absorb. You can arrange the information in a table to help the reader see the figures at a glance (see Exhibit 7.3). Although this method presents the information in a convenient form, it offers little visual interpretation of the data to assist the reader in understanding what it may mean.

Exhibit 7.3   Sample Table

Table 1.1—Drug Users in Treatment Groups–1990 and 1995

Age Group	Percent of Total	
	1990	1995
13–18	42%	35%
19–29	21%	43%
30–45	15%	12%
45+	22%	10%

Suppose you wanted to present the information more graphically to underscore a point about the success of enrolling members of the 19-to-29-year-old age group in drug treatment programs. A bar chart would enable the reader to see which groups increased at the fastest rate (see Exhibit 7.4A).

On the other hand, suppose you wanted to show that the 19-to-29-year-old age group accounts for an increasing percentage of the total population of drug treatment users. A pie or circle chart would be the best choice to illustrate your point (see Exhibit 7.4B). Each group is represented by a wedge in the circle. This format enables the reader to grasp quickly how much the 19-to-29-year-old age group has increased in five years.

If you want to depict changes in the various age groups over time, you would use the line graph, which depicts the steady progression of change over a fixed period of time (see Exhibit 7.4C). You can explain in your text why the upsurge in enrollment of 19-to-29-year-olds occurred and why enrollment of 13-to-18-years-olds declined.

Finally, you can use symbols to show changes in group enrollment to give the reader a better grasp of how large the increases and decreases are in a more dramatic way. (See Exhibit 7.4D). Your text may be used to emphasize the implications of the data shown in the chart or graph. For example, people aged 19 to 29 who enroll in drug treatment programs are likely to need child support services, as well. Those in older age categories are less likely to have as many infants and small children.

Common Errors

The guidelines below can help you avoid the most common mistakes proposal writers make when using illustrations. The two most common errors are using too many illustrations and not explaining illustrations well enough.

1. *Use only the graphics essential to the proposal text.*
   Unfortunately, many proposal developers believe that if a few graphics are good, more are better. They use so many charts, tables, and graphs that they overwhelm the text. Use only those graphics that emphasize a point, explain key facts in the text, or help the reader remember essential information.

Exhibit 7.4 A–D   Graphic Presentation of Tabular Data

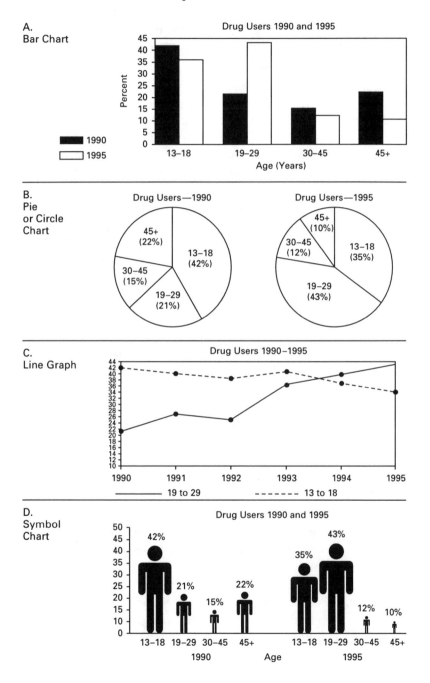

A.
Bar Chart

Drug Users 1990 and 1995

B.
Pie
or Circle
Chart

C.
Line Graph

D.
Symbol
Chart

2. *Make sure all your graphics and tables are designed to the same scale.* Avoid broad discrepancies in size between one graphic and another—for example, a line graph that takes up a quarter page and a circle chart that takes up a full page. Use the same scale to create all charts.

3. *Be sure the terms you use in the graphic or table are the same terms used in the text.* This point is particularly critical when developing proposals for international clients. If you talk about kilometers in the text, don't use miles in the table. If you are copying the graphic from another source, adapt the terms so they are consistent with your test (for example, change Celsius to Fahrenheit).

4. *Use your best judgment when constructing three-dimensional (3-D) charts.* The general rule of thumb is make sure the 3-D feature makes it easier—not harder—for the reader to grasp the information presented in the graphic. Three-dimensional circle charts are fine, but line charts in 3-D can be confusing to the eye. You don't want your graphics to confuse, distract, or frustrate your client.

5. *Cite the graphic or table in the text as close to the relevant information as possible.* Let the reader know the graphic exists early in the relevant paragraph. Don't wait until the next page to mention it.

6. *Be consistent with the format you use to set up tables, charts, and graphs.* If your company has an established format for illustrations, follow it closely. If they do not, create a format and make sure every table and illustration is set in the same style. This not only helps to eliminate confusion but makes your data easier to follow or compare from one illustration or table to the next.

7. *Number all graphics consecutively throughout your paper.* Again, your company may have an established style for numbering tables and illustrations (e.g., Table 1, Table A, Table I, Figure 1.1, Exhibit II, and so on). If there is no established system, set one up and use it throughout the proposal. In general, don't mix tables and figures when numbering sequentially. For example, number tables Table 1, Table 2, and

so on and number figures Figure 1, Figure 2, etc. Avoid mixing tables and figures when numbering illustrations sequentially: Table 1, Figure 2.

8. *Cite your source for the information in each graphic.* If you used government or private research other than your own, cite the source in a footnote at the bottom of the illustration. Find out if you need permission to use the information or if there are other restrictions on usage.

Interpreting Illustrations

It is not enough simply to insert graphics into your proposal. Your readers need to know what the graphics mean, and *you* must interpret the data for them. For the data on groups enrolling in drug treatment programs, for example, don't merely restate the figures in the text. Tell the readers why the changes are meaningful or important. Are treatment programs for the 30-and-above age groups declining, receiving fewer referrals, failing the enrollees, graduating more people than they enroll? Does the increase in the 19-to-29 age group represent the success of a drug treatment outreach program, an increase in funding for programs, better reporting methods, or a larger percentage of the population reaching that age group?

Whenever you include an illustration in your proposal, ask yourself if you have interpreted the data adequately or simply inserted it into the text.

DESIGNING TABLES, CHARTS, AND GRAPHS

Although each form of table, chart, and graph has its own requirements, there are a few general guidelines for designing effective illustrations.

- All illustrations should be identified by number and title. This enables the reader to grasp quickly the main point of the illustration and where in the text it is likely to fall.
- All elements of the illustration should be properly labelled. In the line chart, for example, label all lines clearly so the reader can easily distinguish them.

- Keep the number of colors or patterns to a minimum in any one illustration. Too many colors or patterns are confusing to the eye and obscure your data.
- If you use keys, or legends, to the graphic and any notes containing explanations or source citations, place them below the graphic or in a position that does not obscure any part of the illustration.

Tables—Showing Numbers

Tables are particularly useful for displaying numbers in columns. They have the added advantage of being easy to produce on either a typewriter or computer.

- A table has at least two columns, with headings on the sides and tops of the columns to indicate what the figures represent.
- If the table contains a long series of items you can make it easier to read by arranging the data into groups of two, three, or four lines; by highlighting every other line; or by inserting lines between groups of columns.
- Single-space rows of numbers within tables, but double-space between groups of data and between the headings and the first row of figures.
- All figures in a table are aligned on the right. Commas, decimal points, dollar or percentage signs, and other symbols are aligned vertically. In most cases, numbers should be rounded to the nearest hundredth; that is, they should not extend further than two places to the right of the decimal point.

The examples in Exhibit 7.5A–C show some of the ways that tables can be prepared.

Bar Charts—Showing Relationships Among Groups

Bar or column charts depict relationships among groups of information, such as the number of kilowatts of energy produced in different states over the past 10 years. Bars can be arranged vertically or horizontally.

Exhibit 7.5 A–C Sample Tables

Table A. Composition of Household Garbage—1970 to 2000

Materials	1970 Millions tons/yr	1970 % of Total	1990 Millions tons/yr	1990 % of Total	2000* Millions tons/yr	2000* % of Total
Paper/paperboard	35.4	33.1%	47.9	37.2%	63.1	41.0%
Glass	12.1	11.3%	12.5	9.7%	11.7	7.6%
Metals	13.1	12.3%	12.4	9.6%	13.9	9.0%
Plastics	2.9	2.7%	9.3	7.2%	15.1	9.8%
Rubber/leather	2.9	2.7%	3.2	2.5%	3.7	2.4%
Textiles	2.2	2.1%	2.7	2.1%	3.4	2.2%
Wood	3.8	3.6%	4.9	3.8%	5.9	3.8%
Food wastes	12.3	11.5%	10.5	8.1%	10.4	6.8%
Yard wastes	20.4	19.1%	23.1	17.9%	23.6	15.3%
Other	1.8	1.7%	2.4	1.9%	3.1	2.0%
Totals	106.9	100.0%	128.9	100.0%	153.9	100.0%

*Projected
Source: Environmental Protection Agency

Table B. Threatened and Endangered Species in the World—1993

Category	Endangered U.S.	Endangered Foreign	Threatened U.S.	Threatened Foreign	Species Total*
Mammals	43	237	7	24	311
Birds	73	136	12	2	223
Reptiles	9	55	19	15	98
Amphibians	4	7	6	2	19
Fishes	39	9	33	2	83
Snails	4	2	6	1	13
Clams	27	3	1	1	32
Crustaceans	4	2	2	3	11
Insects	8	2	7	2	19
Plants	134	3	36	4	177
Total	345	456	129	56	986

*Some species are listed as both "endangered" and "threatened."
Source: Fish and Wildlife Service

Table C. 1993 Crimes by Weapon

Category	Firearms	Knife	Personal*	Other	Total
Murder	56.1%	21.5%	7.7%	14.7%	100.0%
Robbery	36.3%	14.5%	43.6%	N/A	94.4%
Aggravated assault	22.3%	23.5%	25.2%	29.0%	100.0%

 * Hands, feet, etc.   N/A = Not Available
   Includes murders where   Note: Percentages may not add
   weapon was unknown   up to 100% due to rounding.

Source: FBI, "Crime in the United States." Washington D.C.: Superintendent of Documents, 1993.

Most computer spreadsheet and graphics programs can be used to create these charts easily.

Stack bar charts show data in segments of a bar and compare one segmented bar to another. These types of bar charts must be clearly labelled to avoid confusing the reader. Generally, limit the number of segments per bar to five or fewer and use colors that are not similar to one another to distinguish each segment. Avoid using similar shades of green, for example. Instead use green, yellow, and blue to mark segments in a stack chart.

When making a bar chart, be sure to label each bar clearly. Avoid creating labels in such a way that the reader has to rotate the page to read the information. Exhibit 7.6A–B shows the preferred way to construct these charts.

Circle Charts—Showing Relationship to the Whole

Circle charts are particularly useful when you want to show the relative sizes of groups compared to the whole. Circle charts show the reader at a glance the proportion of each slice to each other slice and to the whole. In general, limit the number of segments to ten or fewer. If you try to pack too many segments into the circle, it will be difficult to distinguish one segment from another. Spreadsheet and graphic computer programs can be used to construct circle charts quickly.

Circle charts can also be used to show progressive changes over time and to compare the changes in each segment as well as in the whole. Exhibit 7.7A–C demonstrates the different uses of circle charts.

Line Charts—Showing Trends over Time

Line charts allow readers to see trends in data over time. Although computer programs can construct line charts, keep these principles in mind:

- Keep the number of lines in the chart to five or fewer.
- Label all lines clearly. Use different patterns or colors that easily distinguish one line from another.
- Label the horizontal and vertical scales clearly.

Exhibit 7.8A–C illustrates different types of line charts.

Exhibit 7.6 A–B   Sample Bar Charts

A.
Horizontal
Bar Chart

Comparison of U.S. and Foreign Voter Participation—1993

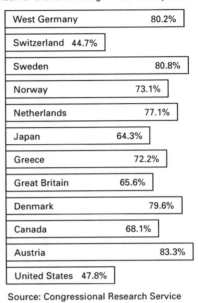

West Germany	80.2%
Switzerland	44.7%
Sweden	80.8%
Norway	73.1%
Netherlands	77.1%
Japan	64.3%
Greece	72.2%
Great Britain	65.6%
Denmark	79.6%
Canada	68.1%
Austria	83.3%
United States	47.8%

Source: Congressional Research Service

B.
Vertical
Bar Chart

Career Diplomats Versus Political Appointments—1961–1993

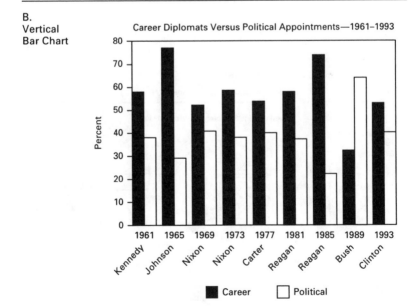

Source: Senate Foreign Relations Committee

Exhibit 7.7 A–C   Sample Circle Charts

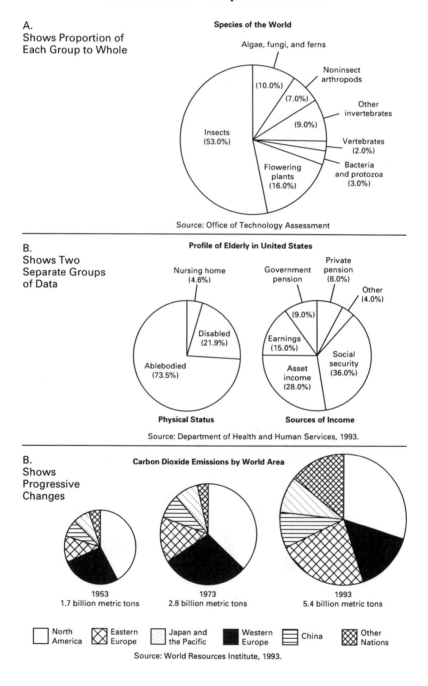

A.
Shows Proportion of
Each Group to Whole

Species of the World

Algae, fungi, and ferns
(10.0%)

Noninsect arthropods
(7.0%)

Other invertebrates
(9.0%)

Insects
(53.0%)

Vertebrates
(2.0%)

Bacteria and protozoa
(3.0%)

Flowering plants
(16.0%)

Source: Office of Technology Assessment

B.
Shows Two
Separate Groups
of Data

Profile of Elderly in United States

Nursing home
(4.6%)

Disabled
(21.9%)

Ablebodied
(73.5%)

Physical Status

Government pension

Private pension
(8.0%)

Other
(4.0%)

(9.0%)

Earnings
(15.0%)

Social security
(36.0%)

Asset income
(28.0%)

Sources of Income

Source: Department of Health and Human Services, 1993.

B.
Shows
Progressive
Changes

Carbon Dioxide Emissions by World Area

1953
1.7 billion metric tons

1973
2.8 billion metric tons

1993
5.4 billion metric tons

North America   Eastern Europe   Japan and the Pacific   Western Europe   China   Other Nations

Source: World Resources Institute, 1993.

Exhibit 7.8 A–C   Sample Line Charts

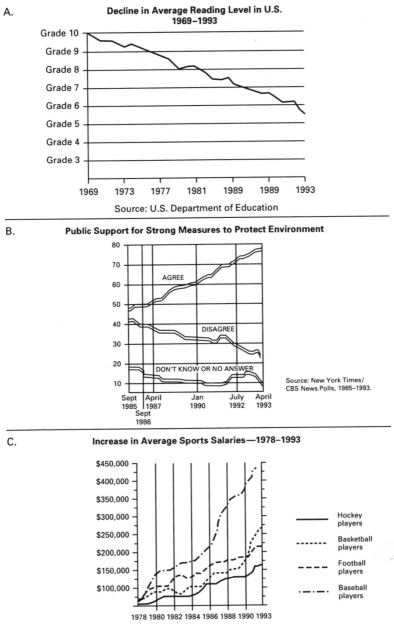

A.

Decline in Average Reading Level in U.S.
1969–1993

Source: U.S. Department of Education

B.   **Public Support for Strong Measures to Protect Environment**

AGREE

DISAGREE

DON'T KNOW OR NO ANSWER

Sept   April   Jan   July   April
1985   1987   1990   1992   1993
        Sept
        1986

Source: New York Times/
CBS News Polls, 1985–1993.

C.   **Increase in Average Sports Salaries—1978–1993**

Hockey
players

Basketball
players

Football
players

Baseball
players

1978 1980 1982 1984 1986 1988 1990 1993

Source: Sports League of America, 1993

Pictorial or Symbol Graphics—Showing Data in Visual Form

Some of the more common pictorial or symbol graphics include organizational and flow charts, maps, photographs, diagrams, and paintings. Organizational charts and flow charts are commonly used in business publications, including proposals. In preparing these graphics, use the following guidelines:

- The symbols should be easy to identify. If you are using the symbol of a machine to represent equipment sales figures, for example, be sure the machine is easy to recognize.
- The symbols should accurately represent differences in size or percentages; their size should be in direct proportion to the amounts they are supposed to represent.
- Label all important elements on an organizational or flow chart, map, diagram, photograph, etc.
- Avoid packing too much information into the illustration. Simplify the chart or picture as much as possible and use the text to elaborate.
- Put any explanations or source notes at the bottom of the illustration.

Exhibit 7.9A–C shows examples of pictorial charts.

Exhibit 7.9 A–C   Sample Pictorial Graphics

**A.
Sample
Organizational
Chart**

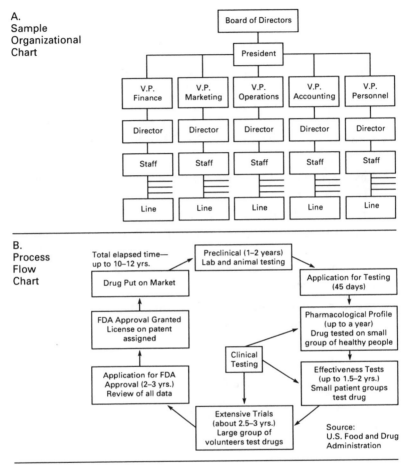

**B.
Process
Flow
Chart**

**C.
Sample Pictorial Chart**

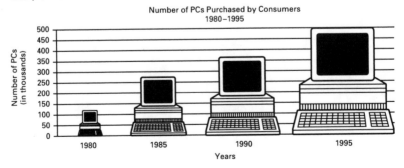

Final Checklist

No matter how rushed the production schedule, make sure you build in time to check through the document carefully before you submit it to the client. Use this checklist to guard against errors.

☐ Has the document been proofread carefully one final time? If possible, have someone proof it who has not seen the document up to this point. Sometimes a new eye catches obvious mistakes everyone else has missed. In one instance, a proofreader noticed that the client's name had been misspelled on the title page.

☐ Has the numbering of pages and the sequencing of tables and figures been double-checked? Make sure the pages cited in the table of contents are accurate.

☐ Have the latest versions of illustrations, graphics, and appendix material been included? When proposals go through several revisions, it is easy for the wrong version of a graphic to turn up in the document.

☐ Are there any missing pages, illustrations turned the wrong way, appendices listed but not included?

☐ Is the printing of an acceptable quality? Check for blurred print, fuzzy images, or other printing irregularities.

☐ Will the binding hold the document securely?

Now that your proposal has passed this final inspection, all that remains to be done is to present the proposal to the client. Chapter 8 discusses ways to develop a winning presentation.

CHAPTER
≡ EIGHT

MAKING CLIENT PRESENTATIONS

Tracy Masters stopped by Ed Breen's desk.

"BioCom wants us to do a presentation next Friday. Ms. Reiner just got word from the vice president at BioCom."

Breen turned noticeably paler. "Will *we* have to give part of the presentation?"

"You bet. Right after the technical team. Apparently BioCom was impressed by our initial work on the marketing strategy. They want to hear more."

"But . . . I'm lousy at speaking in front of people."

Masters laughed in sympathy.

"Don't worry. You should see the schedule Ms. Reiner has drawn up for developing the presentation. We'll have so many practice sessions we'll be able to do this talk backwards."

"I have to admit, we do have a really good program design for this project."

"Then it's time to tell BioCom all about it."

•　•　•

STEP 9: PRESENTING THE PROPOSAL TO THE CLIENT

In some instances, you will be asked to make a presentation of your proposal to the client. Whether you realize it or not, a client presentation is actually a sales talk. You are selling the client on three major points:

1. You have a thorough understanding of the client's situation.

2. You have the best solution for the client's needs.

3. Your firm is the best one to do the job.

The client must be convinced that all three points are true. Otherwise, another company is likely to get the project.

Good presentations are a matter of planning, organization, and practice, combined with that elusive quality known as presence, luck, right timing, chemistry, or whatever else it may be called. It is that special rapport you bring to the presentation that tells the client you have absolute confidence in your solution and your company.

In this chapter we give you some basic guidelines about how to prepare and deliver your presentation. We also include a few tips on how to prepare for success and how to handle troublesome questions from the client audience.

PLANNING STEPS

Good planning is a critical element of success in any presentation you give. In general, you will need to be prepared in the following four areas:

- A talk given by one or more of your staff members outlining the main points of the proposal. The client audience may or may not ask questions during this time.
- The use of graphics and other visuals (transparencies, charts, handouts, slides, and other aids) to illustrate and clarify the main points.
- A question-and-answer time during which the client audience will quiz you about the proposal's features and your company's capabilities.
- A wrap-up time in which you will review the main selling points and try to convince the client that your firm should be selected for the project.

The planning stage begins by answering four basic questions: why are we giving this presentation, who are we giving it to, what do we plan to say, and where and when do we give the presentation?

Why Are You Giving the Presentation?

At first, the answer seems obvious: The client requested it and you want to win the bid. But it's worth your while to look deeper and to establish an *objective* for your talk. Every effective presentation is founded on a clear objective.

A presentation can do one or all of the following:

- Educate or inform
- Propose recommendations and gain acceptance
- Initiate action
- Evoke interest
- Interpret, clarify, evaluate
- Introduce new ideas
- Sell or persuade

These objectives are rather general, and you probably want to achieve a combination of them. But what specifically are you seeking to accomplish in the relatively short time you will have with the client? Take time to put your objectives in writing. A written objective can provide a unifying theme for your entire presentation. Use "to" phrases to state your objectives: to convince, to persuade, to demonstrate, to inform. For example, the objectives below give the presentation teams a clear idea of their common goals:

- To convince BioCom that our company offers a superior software product as well as a sound marketing strategy to capture a significant share of this software market.

- To prove to FairValue Hardware that by improving customer service—as well as upgrading major stores—the company can regain its market share and overcome strong competition from rival chains.

- To demonstrate to South Holland Community Hospital that our company's outreach program will attract key patient groups, improve the hospital's financial standing, and create an ongoing need for the hospital's services in the surrounding community above and beyond immediate care facilities.

Writing a good objective is not easy. One way to facilitate the process is to visualize what you want to happen at the end of your presentation. What information do you most want the client to remember? What impression do you want to create about your solution and your company? What decisions do you want the client to make?

As you write your objective, keep three criteria in mind: Your objective must be attainable, measurable, and realistic. You may be trying to attain too many objectives in one talk. Remember, the more objectives you have, the more tasks are required to accomplish them. Keep the objective simple.

The results of your presentation should be measurable. In the case of a proposal presentation, the measurement yardstick is straightforward: The client accepted your solution and hired your company.

Who Is the Client Audience?

You began the proposal writing process by looking at the situation from the client's perspective. This orientation is even more important when it comes to presenting your ideas in person. To do the most effective job, you must know your audience. In general, companies are interested in five main areas:

- reducing costs
- increasing return on investment
- saving time
- improving quality and performance
- raising productivity

If you can identify which of these are of *primary* concern to the client, you will begin to mesh your objective with the needs of your audience. BioCom, for instance, may be interested primarily in raising productivity and increasing their return on investment. The objective of providing them with superior software and a marketing strategy speaks to both these needs.

In addition, your background research on the client, and all client contacts that the proposal manager and team have had, will be invaluable when you start preparing for the presentation. This information will tell you who in the client organization is likely to be resistant to your ideas, who may be supportive, and who are the major decision makers.

Go over your checklists and background notes to determine what appears to motivate the client management. What is the tone and philosophy of the organizational culture? Does the client see itself as an innovator, conservative, socially minded, or strictly business oriented?

The answers to these and other questions will help you to determine how to tailor your presentation to match the characteristics and communication style of your client. For example, if the client president is detail oriented and you spend all your time on the broad picture, the client is likely to perceive you as too vague or as promising too much without explaining how it will all happen.

This planning step is more important than you may think. Many outstanding proposal ideas die on the presentation floor simply because the proposal team forgot about tailoring its talk to the client's needs.

The proposal manager and the company's liaison to the client must work closely together to develop an effective way to communicate the proposal to the client.

What Do You Plan to Say?

By this time you have established your objective and know a great deal about your intended audience. Having put the proposal together, you also know your topic. At this point, you can ask yourself a few questions to help focus your thinking.

- What does the client already know about this topic?
- What else does the client want to know about it?
- What does the client *need* to know?
- What *doesn't* the client need to know?
- What topics or areas should we avoid?

This is the point to begin separating what the client *needs* to know from what is simply *nice* to know. For example, BioCom management needs to know the salient features of the software program, but does it need to know how much trouble it was to create it or how the software team solved each problem? Probably not. Only BioCom's technical staff is likely to be interested in such details.

The last two points—what the client doesn't need to know and what areas you should avoid—refer to sensitive issues. These are areas that you generally don't want to bring up in the presentation but are prepared to handle should the question-and-answer session reveal them. For instance, if the BioCom software program is going to require a more complicated interface between computers and printers, the Andover team may not want to discuss this issue at the presentation. If the client brings it up, however, they can simply say they are working on several options to simplify the problem.

When and Where Is the Presentation?

For planning purposes, you need to have a firm idea of when and where the presentation is to be given. You then know how much lead time you have to develop the talk. If possible, make up a floor plan of the room where the presentation will be held. This will help you plan where to place your visual aids and what seating arrangements you may encounter. In many instances, however, you may not know exactly where you will be speaking until the day of the presentation.

By knowing the location in advance, you can estimate how much travel time to allow for yourselves and your materials. You should devise one or two alternate routes or forms of transportation that can be used should the unexpected happen. One group of consultants, for example, found its route to the client's office blocked by fire trucks. Luckily, the consultants had planned another route and were able to make the meeting with only a few minutes' delay.

ORGANIZING THE PRESENTATION

Once the initial planning steps are complete, you can begin organizing your presentation. You will need to organize the text of your talk and the visual aids you are going to use. In some cases, your presentation may also involve a live demonstration or the use of interactive media. Regardless of the simplicity or sophistication of your proposal topic, however, there are a few basic principles that will help you organize your materials and your team to make an effective proposal presentation.

Organizing the Topic

You have already organized your topic for the written proposal. But an oral presentation involves more than simply reading what you wrote. You need to use an organizational approach tailored to captivate an audience's interest and hold its attention throughout the talk. Here are some well-known organizational techniques that should fit your situation:

- The Problem-Solution Approach. Start with the current situation (what your client's problems or needs are), move to your solution, and finish with a picture of what the company will gain from adopting your solution.

- The Descriptive Approach. Begin by describing your solution to client's problem or need, then explain what your solution will accomplish, and how it will do so.

- The Best Alternative Approach. Lay out the client's problem or need, offer several possible alternatives, then explain why the alternative you chose is the best one for the client's situation.
- The Events Approach. Explain what happened that created the client's problem or need, why it happened, and how you will help the client address it.
- The Technical Approach. Discuss the client's problem, your approach to the problem, the results the client can expect adopting your approach, and your conclusions and recommendations.

Once you decide on an approach, you can do a rough draft of your presentation either in list form, as an outline, or on visuals such as transparencies, slides, or charts (also known as storyboards, which show a visual on the top half and text on the bottom half of a chart or page). This will give a good idea of the main points you want to cover and help you to distinguish between nice-to-know and need-to-know items.

The goal at this stage is to divide your talk into several subtopics. For example, the Andover team might divide its BioCom presentation into the following topic areas:

1. BioCom's needs and vision for a uniform medical reporting format and the problems they have identified.
2. Current state-of-the-art medical format software and its limitations.
3. Andover's study of the software problems and its experience and successes with similar software.
4. The software Andover has developed, its features, advantages, and results.
5. A marketing strategy for BioCom to take advantage of the new software and become a leader in this field.
6. A wrap-up listing recommendations and results BioCom can achieve with the new software and marketing strategy.

By dividing the topic into categories, you can develop a concise, informative outline that addresses all the main points without bogging you down in excessive detail. At this stage, you may want to assign a rough time limit to each topic. In the case above, topics one through three may take only about one-quarter of the time, topics four and five about one-half, and the final wrap-up only about one-quarter. The question-and-answer session would follow.

To keep yourself focused on your objective and outline, ask yourself at each stage of developing your talk "What does the client absolutely *have* to know about his area? What is important to the client? What can we let go?" This entire process is a series of choices, made within the context of limited time and the need to sustain client interest.

Creating Text and Visual Aids

Once you have established your main points and developed your text, you must think about the best combination of text and visual aids to convey your presentation. The actual physical form of the talk you take with you to the presentation will depend a great deal on the individual situation. In some cases, you may be able to use index cards with key facts written on each card. In other cases, overhead transparencies and a script may be all you will need. In still other instances, the talk may be divided among several people, each one of whom will have his or her own notes, slides, or outlines.

Index cards have the advantage of being easy to delete or amend on the spot. They are relatively unobtrusive, and can be easily slipped into a pocket or briefcase. You can key them to overhead transparencies, slides, or storyboards and use them to jog your memory should you be distracted or forget to cover an essential fact.

Visuals are essential to any presentation. A study conducted by the Wharton School of Business at the University of Pennsylvania proved that presenters using visuals were judged by their audiences as being more professional, persuasive, and credible. Exhibit 8.1 summarizes the advantages and disadvantages of using various forms of visual aids. Use this information as a guide to help you select the best visual forms for each presentation you may be called upon to do.

The key element to keep in mind is that visual aids should supplement or enhance your presentation, not serve as the main focus or substitute for content that should be communicated verbally. Nor should you overwhelm the audience with so many visuals that your main points are lost in a blizzard of color, design, and show-stopping special effects. Use the visual aids for maximum impact, keeping the style and character of your audience in mind.

Exhibit 8.1   Advantages and Disadvantages of Various Visual Aids

Visual Aid	Advantage	Disadvantage
Marker boards chalk boards	Easy to obtain and use; little or no cost	Dull; low visibility; limits audience size
Flip charts	Easy to make and use; good audience interaction	Low visual impact; wear and tear with use
Overhead transparencies	Quick and economical; easy to carry and store; projectors available for any size audience; easy to alter or redo	Mechanics of switching visuals can be distracting; projectors can block audience view
Slides	Higher quality than overheads; projectors easy to carry and use; high visual impact; long life	Darkened room required decreases contact with audience; slides cannot be redone easily; can be expensive
Films, videotape	Both have high visual impact and high interest level; suit any size audience; video easier to produce	Audience focuses on visuals instead of speaker; film is expensive and takes time to produce; video may require special playback equipment, particularly in foreign countries
Models, mockup, props	High impact value; add reality to presentation	Can be costly and time-consuming to prepare; may limit size of audience
Video teleconferencing	Connects two or more locations; saves time and money; enables audience to reach decisions more quickly	Can be costly and requires full-time staff to set up and maintain the system
Electronic presentations	Computer-prepared charts can be shown directly on a monitor screen; cost effective, changes are easy to make	Cost of equipment can be high; requires highly trained staff; may be available for small audiences only

One traditional drawback in creating visual aids—the expense—has been largely overcome by modern computer technology. With the current advances in graphics software and the new generation of laser printers, virtually everyone can make professional-looking transparencies, charts, and slides for their presentations at a reasonable cost.

Organizing Your Team

All team members should know exactly what they are supposed to do for the presentation and when and how they are supposed to do it. This task can be accomplished by creating a matrix that shows which topics are assigned to which team members. If during the development process one team member feels more comfortable with another topic, you can make adjustments. Be sure to have backup team members available among your staff should any team member be unable to perform his or her part of the presentation due to illness, accident, or family emergencies.

It's also a good idea to make each team member responsible for handling client questions about his or her particular area. In this manner, you can direct the client's questions to the person on your team who is the most qualified to answer them. This also frees the other team members to concentrate on their area of expertise and gives the client the impression that you are conducting an effective, well-coordinated company effort.

Taking Care of the Details

Part of organizing your presentation involves such details as remembering extension cords, extra markers, spare light bulbs for the projector, scissors, tape, and the countless other supplies you need to support your talk. Draw up a list of the items you must have and put one or two team members in charge of making sure these items are brought to the presentation. *Do not assume that the client will be able to supply what you need.* In fact, if you have to ask, it may damage the professional image you wish to convey. Pay attention to the details.

PRACTICING THE PRESENTATION

Before you go in front of the client, you will need to practice your presentation, usually several times, until you have it down cold. This usually involves at least the following:

- practicing to refine each talk given by team members
- roleplaying with a critical audience
- dress rehearsals
- learning how to relax

Practicing Individual Talks

Notecards, outlines, and visual aids are one thing. Standing up in front of an audience and actually giving the talk is quite another. You need to move smoothly from one point to the next, while coordinating visual aids with your talk—bringing them in at just the right time and changing them when you want to emphasize a point.

All team members should practice their individual talks with other team members to refine the content and to coordinate visual aids. You may find that the talk needs more illustration or less. If someone else is going to work the transparencies or the slide projector or turn the flip charts for you as you speak, how will it be done? Where will the screen and equipment be? How will you signal one another when the right moment occurs?

These details must be worked out well before the talk is given. Once you have a system established, you can adjust it to meet changing conditions. Expecting your partner to intuit when and where to change a visual aid is an invitation to disaster.

Roleplaying with a Live Audience

Once the individual talks have been refined by the team, the entire presentation should be given in front of an in-house management audience. The audience's role is to critique the presentation and provide realistic feedback for the team. If you know you will have a problem with one area of your presentation, the audience can act as the client and grill the team on that area until you are satisfied you can handle any client objections.

It may be grueling to endure such a critiquing session, but it is far better for your own management to find the flaws in your presentation than for the client to do so. Go into these sessions with the idea that you are developing a draft of your talk. The whole purpose of rough drafts is to rip them apart to find the flaws and to make the presentation stronger. The more you can detach your ego from your work, the better your work is likely to become.

Dress Rehearsals

The final practice stage involves putting all the talks and visual aids together in a setting that resembles the actual client meeting room as closely as possible. This enables you to develop the best arrangement of seating, equipment, and speaker position. Exhibit 8.2 shows examples of different arrangements you may encounter. Notice that the illustrations in the figure show you how to set up your visual equipment so that all members of the audience can easily see the screen, board, or charts. Remember to give careful thought to such matters as glare from windows, the location of electrical outlets, outside noises that might intrude, and so on.

The easier you make it for the client audience to see and hear you without distraction, the more of their attention you'll have.

Learning How to Relax

Most people faced with the prospect of speaking in front of others experience the pounding heart, sweaty palms, and nervous tics typical of fear. In a proposal presentation, you have the added pressure of knowing that an entire job may hang on the outcome of your performance. It's enough to arouse stark terror even in seasoned presenters.

However, there is a secret to how to manage your fear of public speaking. Notice we said *manage,* not *eliminate.* It's not possible to eliminate all the fear you may feel. But you can learn to manage your emotions enough to find yourself more relaxed and confident in front of the client.

The secret to managing your fear is this: *It is impossible to be physically relaxed and emotionally terrified at the same time.* By relaxing yourself physically, you will automatically relax emotionally.

Exhibit 8.2   Typical Seating Arrangements

A.
Square Arrangement

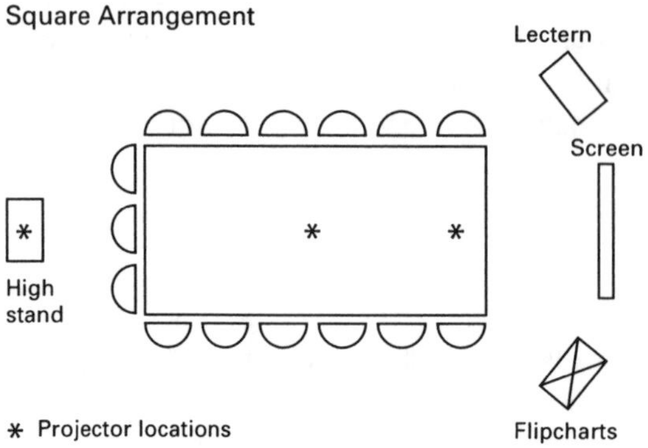

Lectern

Screen

Traditional arrangement with projectors on the table or behind the table, speakers to one side to allow audience to view screen.

High stand

Flipcharts

✳ Projector locations

B.
U-Shaped Arrangement

Lectern

Screen

Projector tables

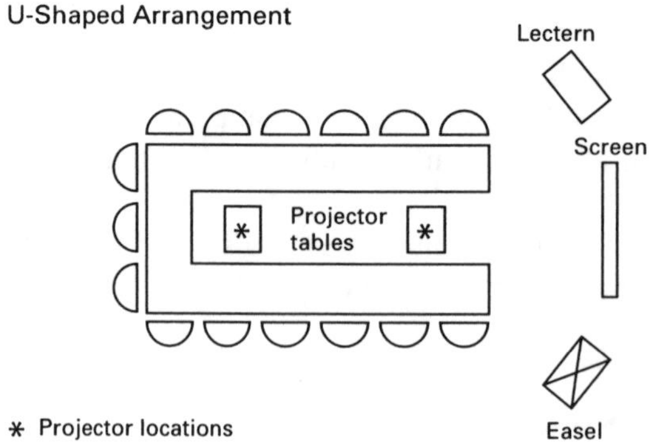

U-shaped arrangement allows projectors to be placed in center— speaker and screen are clearly visible to everyone in the audience.

✳ Projector locations

Easel

C.
U-Shaped Arrangement

Screen

Lectern

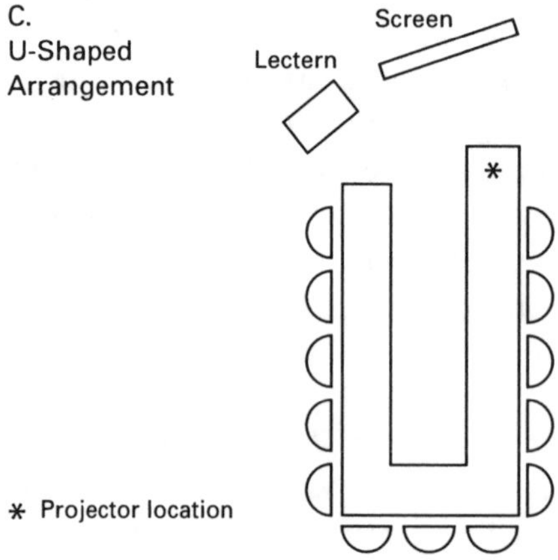

In this arrangement, the projector is placed to one side, forcing speaker to turn the screen. Audience on far side may see a slightly distorted image.

✳ Projector location

Follow these three guidelines:

1. Breathe. When people are frightened, their breathing becomes shallow and rapid. When you change your breathing and take slower, deeper breaths, you are signalling your nervous system that the situation is not life-threatening. Your body begins to relax.

2. Move. Physical activity burns up the stress hormones released by strong fear. Before the talk, move around, take a brief walk, stretch your muscles. If you are seated, tense and relax your muscles. Check to see whether you are tensing your neck and shoulders, your jaw, your stomach muscles—if so, relax them.

3. Get support. Agree beforehand to support each other in the presentation. Use inspirational phrases, self-talk, whatever provides emotional support to you in moments of stress. In the talk, when you feel yourself becoming too anxious, look at the designated friendly face. Emotional support is physically reassuring and will help your body relax.

Keep these three steps in mind throughout the practice sessions so they will be part of your pre-presentation warmup. Write *Breathe, Move, Get support* on your index cards or script so you will have a visual cue during your part of the presentation.

Remember, when your physical body relaxes, the rest of you relaxes.

SURVIVAL TIPS

Give yourself an added edge in the presentation by taking a few extra precautions. You want to set up the room so that you know everything is in order for the talk. You also want to be prepared to handle resistance or even hostile reactions the client may throw your way.

Checklist: Setting Up for Success

Here is a quick checklist of steps to take when you arrive at the client's place of business.

- ☐ Arrange to be allowed into the meeting room early. Plan to arrive half an hour before the talk. This gives you time to adjust to any unexpected situations you may find when you arrive (e.g., a blind corner in the room, construction noise outside, etc.).

- ☐ Check the physical surroundings of the room. Can you change the order of seats around the tables, rearrange the tables themselves, close the curtains or blinds, or do other tasks to arrange the room for the best presentation?

- ☐ If the client is to supply you with any equipment—video monitors, projectors, etc.—are they in the room and do they work?

- ☐ Check all equipment to be sure it works properly. Project a slide or transparency to be sure it can be seen from all areas of the room where client personnel will be sitting. Check the sound level of microphones or video/film materials.

- ☐ Check your materials to make sure they are in the right order, that nothing has been damaged in transit, and that everything is right-side up.

- ☐ Avoid eating a big meal or drinking cold liquids before your talk. Both items tend to affect the throat and interfere with proper speaking.

- ☐ Go over the schedule of your presentation one last time with all team members.

If despite your best efforts things still go wrong (the slide won't pop up, your partner puts up the wrong transparency, a flip chart falls to the floor), stay calm. The more you take such minor disasters in stride, the more your audience will as well. Have a contingency plan in mind should things go wrong.

Above all, don't call attention to the mistake by blowing up at your partner, obsessing on the missing slide or transparency, or making too much of the error. *Move on.* Chances are your audience won't think twice about it if you simply go on to the next point. They may even admire your grace under pressure.

Handling Troublesome Questions

What happens when your worst fears are confirmed and the person you thought would cause a problem actually does? Trouble can come in many forms—from mildly voiced objections to outright hostility from someone in the audience. Here are a few suggestions to help you turn the situation to your advantage.

First and foremost, *remain calm.* If your questioner can provoke you, he or she has won the round whether you offer a rebuttal or not. Buy yourself a little time if you need to calm down. Take a drink of water, walk to the other side of the speaker's area, adjust the microphone. Remember to focus on the issue, not the person who raised it.

Receive all questions cordially. Statements such as, "That's a good question . . ." or "That's a common concern . . ." help defuse the situation and put it on more neutral footing.

Listen carefully to the question. Have you really heard what the person is saying or are you distracted by who is saying it or how they are saying it? Listen to the words and the underlying intention. Ask for clarifications if you are not sure you understand the issue being raised.

Avoid flip or off-the-cuff answers. Again, buying yourself a little time—a few seconds may be all you need—will give you a chance to ask yourself:

- Why is this question being asked? Perhaps you were not clear about the point.

- How does it fit into the objectives of our presentation? Is the question an opportunity to promote your main points once again?

- Can I give a concise, clear answer? Is there an efficient way to answer the question without appearing curt or flippant?

Avoid trying to impress or please your audience with a fast rejoinder. A little thought can turn the situation to your favor.

If you don't know an answer, say so—or refer the question to a team member who does know. "That's an excellent point. Brad Shaw is our expert in that area. Brad, what would you say?"

Keep the statements "I" centered instead of "you" centered. Avoid saying "You didn't understand that point." Instead say something like "I'm glad you asked that question," or "That's something we considered and had to reject. Let me clarify."

If a questioner appears to be openly hostile or aggressive toward you or any member of your team, stay focused on the issues. You may be asked loaded questions, hypothetical questions, leading questions, or questions designed to derail your presentation. Here's what the experts suggest:

- Use a bridging technique. Move from the hot issue to one you want to talk about. Good bridging statements include:

  "Quite the contrary. Let me show you how we . . ."

  "I understand that position, however, . . ."

  "We may disagree on that, but a more important point is . . ."

- Follow with positive points you want to emphasize that focus on your objective for making the presentation.

- Question the questioner. Sometimes this tactic will reveal the questioner's real motivation. Maybe they are threatened by the changes you are proposing. Find out more about why the person is asking hostile questions.

- If appropriate, use humor to defuse the situation. In some cases, hostile questions can be the result of circumstances—the room is too hot, the session has been a long one, the material may be difficult to follow. A humorous remark that captures a shared sense of frustration can be enough to lighten the atmosphere and bring the audience back to the main focus. However, be very careful with this technique—you must know your audience and feel confident that the humor won't backfire on you. *Never* make the questioner the butt of the joke.

- Stay in control of the exchange. Where you can agree with the questioner, do so, but bring the focus back to the points you want to make. You want to leave the audience on a strong, positive note.

Checklist for Client Presentations

Prior to your presentation, make a quick list of major points to remember. You might draw up something like the following:

- ☐ Have you established a clear objective for making the presentation?
- ☐ Do you know the client audience and what you need to say to them?
- ☐ Has the time and place for the presentation been confirmed?
- ☐ Have you organized the topic into subtopics?
- ☐ Have you outlined the talk on cards or in a script?
- ☐ Have you selected the best visuals?
- ☐ Does everyone on the team understand what they are to do?
- ☐ Have you listed the details you need to remember?
- ☐ Has the team practiced the talk and conducted a dress rehearsal?
- ☐ Can you arrive early at the client site to arrange the room and check the equipment?
- ☐ Have you strategized how to handle troublesome questions?

This final stage in the 9-step process can be just the beginning for you and your firm. This book has offered you an efficient, effective method to help you evaluate RFPs quickly and to find the best jobs that match your firm's marketing strategy and capabilities. You can establish a sound proposal-writing process in your company to help you highlight your solutions and qualifications in a way that catches the clients' attention. We hope the guidelines, suggestions, and recommendations in the book will assist you in offering your clients the best services possible.

Today, with more people forming their own businesses, competition for clients is intense—and getting hotter all the time. It's up to every entrepreneur to find opportunities or to create them where they may not have existed before. We hope this book helps you along the way. As the adage goes: luck favors the prepared!

APPENDIX
≡A

SAMPLE EXECUTIVE SUMMARY

≡ S AMPLE
E XECUTIVE
S UMMARY

The executive summary in Appendix A is from a medium-sized consulting firm that specializes in helping firms relocate and design their data-processing facilities. Appendix B contains the proposal for this project, and Appendix C shows the resume boilerplates included with the proposal.

In the executive summary, the proposal team emphasizes the client's needs and the solution that Western Consulting Associates has developed. The company focuses on the complete program of services it provides and its accomplishments in this field. The client not only has a good overview of what the proposal contains but also a strong impression of the company.

≡ Executive Summary

INTRODUCTION

Western Consulting Associates proposes a complete program of services to assist Armstrong & Hou Financial, Inc., in the design and construction of a new data-processing center. This program will be accomplished in three phases and will produce deliverable results that meet or exceed all technical requirements set forth in the Request for Proposal. We understand that Armstrong & Hou is working within a very tight schedule to complete the work, and we feel confident our company can meet the three-month timeframe stated in the proposal.

Our three-phase program focuses on the preparation of block diagrams and requirements, detailed requirements for bid specifications, and support for Armstrong & Hou's design and construction bidding process. In addition to providing assistance with the new facility, we also offer Armstrong & Hou continuous support to maintain its data-processing services throughout the relocation and design stages. Western Consulting Associates specializes in maintaining uninterrupted computer services while developing new systems at a relocation site.

OUR APPROACH

The three-phase program that we propose will enable Armstrong & Hou to select the best design for its data center, develop precise specifications for soliciting construction bids, and ensure the most efficient use of the 10,000 to 12,000-square-foot office space purchased in the Chicago area. The data-processing center will be able to provide fully integrated services to all its clients with increased speed and efficiency.

Phase I consists of a close examination of the space requirements to develop the base building and data center designs. This phase also includes establishing criteria for the selection of environmental support equipment and completing specific documents for all facets of construction (e.g., electrical, plumbing, fire protection, and security interfaces).

Phase II involves creating detailed requirements from which Armstrong & Hou's architect and engineer can develop a bid specifications package. Our consultants have devised a particularly time-saving method of determining how to select bids from among those solicited.

Phase III, which will be initiated once Phases I and II have been approved by Armstrong & Hou, consists of support for the firm's design and construction process. We will help Armstrong & Hou staff review bid specifications for conformance to project requirements and adjust the design to the firm's configuration.

To accomplish the tasks in Phases I and II, we will form a joint Western-Armstrong & Hou task force that will report directly to the president of Armstrong & Hou. We will hold weekly review meetings with the firm's staff and work closely with its technical group. Such coordination will enable us to stay on schedule and solve any problems that arise in a timely manner.

PROPOSED PROJECT RESULTS

Once Phase I and II have been completed, we will present Armstrong & Hou with a set of design drawings and requirement books. These include:

- Phase I - Block diagrams of computer room, total loads for computer room, requirements for closets; design development documents and sketches for electrical supply, security, fire protection, and high voltage AC.

- Phase II - One-quarter inch layout and recommended considerations for computer room and adjacent area; list of workstation components; requirements for the raised floor, hung ceiling, and electrical layout; and plans for security, fire protection, high voltage AC, specialty plumbing, and vendor selection.

TIME AND COST OVERVIEW

We anticipate meeting Armstrong & Hou's schedule of completing Phases I and II by October 15 and Phase III five weeks later after receiving approval to proceed with the final stage. Our extensive experience with relocation and design projects often enables us to streamline work tasks without compromising safety or quality.

Our pricing structure is based on standard industry practices of quoting a fee for each phase of the project. Our fees include support for all design work, bid specifications, and vendor selection until the design center is completed. All of-of-pocket expenses incurred by Western Consulting Associates on behalf of Armstrong & Hou will be billed at actual cost.

The proposal pricing, configurations, and terms stated are valid for 60 days from the date on the cover of the proposal.

WESTERN CONSULTING ASSOCIATES

Western Consulting Associates was founded in 1970 to assist firms in the process of relocating and designing their computer and data-processing facilities. Today, our firm is recognized internationally as one of the leading companies in this field. We have pioneered many of the current techniques used to design data center layouts, safeguard power systems, and provide security systems that prevent the loss of key data during transfer. We have experience with a wide range of mainframes and interactive networks used by firms similar to Armstrong & Hou.

The relocation and design of a data-processing facility is a highly complex task that requires an experienced, dedicated team and close coordination between the company staff and consultants. We believe that Western Consulting Associates offers a unique blend of experience, expertise, and custom services to meet Armstrong & Hou's requirements for this project.

APPENDIX
B

SAMPLE PROPOSAL

≡ S AMPLE
P ROPOSAL

The proposal in Appendix B is from a medium-sized consulting firm that specializes in relocation of data-processing facilities. The RFP has requested a proposal for moving the client's facilities from one city to another. Appendix A contains the Executive Summary for this proposal, and Appendix C contains the resume boilerplates that would be included in the document.

Because the project focuses primarily on steps involved in relocating and designing a data-processing facility, the proposal writers use an outline form. This approach makes it easy for the client to see the major steps involved in each phase and what to expect in terms of tasks and results.

For this type of project the technical section consists of the work plan, while the management section is likely to be confined primarily to listing the results, or products, that can be delivered to the client. The time and cost estimates will also be brief. The client can then request a more detailed breakdown of time, cost, and management issues at a later date.

Armstrong & Hou Financial, Inc.   1
Data Center Design

Response to Requirements
DATA CENTER DESIGN

Armstrong & Hou Financial, Inc.
Armstrong International Building
34 Silver Plaza Drive
Alamagordo, TX 50221

Mr. Calvin T. Schwartz
President

Proposal Submitted
by

Western Consulting Associates
142 Riverside Business Court
Houston, TX 56621

Armstrong & Hou Proposal No: 69–002
May 23, 19—

Armstrong & Hou Financial, Inc.   2
Data Center Design

TABLE OF CONTENTS

Armstrong & Hou Financial, Inc.   3
Data Center Design

I. OUR UNDERSTANDING OF THE SITUATION

As a result of our examination of the Request for Proposal and our
conversations with Armstrong & Hou Financial, Inc. Management, we
have developed the following understanding of the company's situation:

- Armstrong & Hou Financial, Inc. presently operates a large scale
  data center in the Armstrong & Hou International Building,
  which services users throughout the country.
- Armstrong & Hou Financial, Inc. plans to relocate this operation
  to a new facility that is located in Chicago. This new facility
  will serve all current user sites.
- The area required for the new center, its environmental support
  equipment, and the associated administrative space will comprise
  about 10,000–12,000 square feet.
- Armstrong & Hou Financial, Inc. Data Center schedule requires
  the completion of block diagrams, loads, and direction for base
  building support services by October 15. Thirty (30) days after
  that date, the architectural and engineering firm of Hanover and
  Wyle will need detailed specifications to prepare its center
  designs and bid packages.

Armstrong & Hou Financial, Inc. is seeking assistance from Western Consulting Associates to help its engineers, architects, and vendors
to expedite the design and construction of the storage, computer support, and machine rooms of this data center. This required assistance
does not include the design of offices, communications cubicles, or
market data service communications controller rooms outside of the
main Computer Room.

Armstrong & Hou Financial, Inc. 4
Data Center Design

II. OBJECTIVES OF THE PROJECT

The proposed project's major objectives are divided into three phases.

Phase I

Prepare a set of block diagrams and requirements to be used to develop the base building and data center designs. Specifically:

— Current and future space requirements

— Decision data for Armstrong & Hou Financial, Inc.'s (AHF) use in selecting environmental support equipment

— Data center design development requirements documents (including architectural, mechanical, electrical, and plumbing approaches, and fire protection and specialized security interfaces).

Phase II

Develop detailed requirements from which AHF's Architect and Engineer can develop a bid specifications package. This includes detailed:

— Architectural requirements

— Mechanical requirements

— Electrical requirements

— Plumbing requirements

— Fire protection requirements

— Security and monitoring requirements.

Phase III

Support AHF's design and construction efforts by:

— Reviewing bid specifications for conformance to project requirements

— Applying enhancements and changes due to AHF computer configuration adjustments.

Armstrong & Hou Financial, Inc.   5
Data Center Design

III. TECHNICAL SECTION

III.1   Phases I–III: Work Plan Summaries

Phase I - Data Center Design Development Requirements

Five essential activities are needed to develop the Data Center requirements and to achieve deliverable results. These activities are:

1. Develop data center space programs based upon current and
    future space requirements and associated work flows.

2. Review data center hardware and adjacent work station layouts
    to address:
    — Projected computer capacity requirements
    — Operational effectiveness
    — Physical security

3. Provide decision data:
    — Identify in business terms the pros and cons associated with
      specific layouts and environmental systems approaches
    — Help to select the design approach

4. Prepare data center design development requirements and block
    diagrams. The following elements are needed. Requirements for:
    — Exterior walls
    — Ramps
    — Ceiling heights
    — Floor loading
    — Uninterrupted power supply
    — Emergency power
    — Routing of mechanical, electrical and telecommunications
    Block Diagram for:
    — Computer rooms
    — Supporting space

Armstrong & Hou Financial, Inc.   6
Data Center Design

5. Conduct weekly process meetings with AHF and its architects and engineers.

Phase II - Data Center Detailed Requirements

Develop work products required by AHF's architects and engineers for their development of the Data Center bid package. This will include:

1. Prepare Phase II work products including detailed
   — Architectural requirements
   — Mechanical requirements
   — Electrical requirements
   — Plumbing requirements
   — Fire protection requirements and
   — Security and monitoring requirements
2. Review work products with AHF.
3. Present to AHF's architects and engineers.

Phase III - Design Monitoring

The activities in this phase will include:

1. Review bid package drawings and specifications for conformance to project scope.
2. Provide comments and present to AHF's architect and engineer.
3. Review proposed AHF modifications to the design requirements resulting from hardware and technology changes and the like and coordinate these changes with the architect and engineer.

Armstrong & Hou Financial, Inc.   7
Data Center Design

III.2   Phases I–III: Work Plan Details

Phase I - Data Center Design Development Requirements

Gather Planning Information

Define Planned Work Flows

Develop planned work flow through each MIS area:

— Computer room

— Adjacent office area

— Adjacent storage and work areas

Develop Initial Program Estimates

- Review AHF's assumptions used to arrive at the planned space estimates and evaluate facility requirements in light of those assumptions.
- Develop projections of computer facility requirements based upon:
  — Expected effects of changing technology on facility requirements
  — Space required for hardware transitions
- Identify key cabling distance constraints.

Develop Decision Data

- Develop decision data for selecting the methods for providing computer room power protection, mechanical services, security, and fire suppression considering:
  — Power protection alternatives
  — Installation, maintenance, and equipment cost planning estimates for Halon and dry pipe systems
  — Risks
  — Backup site/contingency plan arrangements
  — Cabling and floor loading requirements
  — Availability of separate base building feeds for electrical, mechanical and telecommunications services

Armstrong & Hou Financial, Inc.   8
Data Center Design

Identify Strategic Decision Issues for Layout

On the basis of information obtained, we will identify strategic decisions that Armstrong & Hou Financial, Inc. must make prior to completing the layout and remaining designs. We already anticipate these decisions will include:

- Level of flexibility to accommodate business and technical changes
- Location of data center
- Level of redundancy
- Level of power protection required (current and future)
- Fire protection

In addition, we expect other issues may arise from our data-gathering efforts. For each issue we will research and articulate alternatives and their pros and cons for AHF's consideration.

3. Present Alternatives for Decision Making

   We will present written and oral materials describing alternatives to facilitate the decision-making process for Armstrong & Hou Financial, Inc.'s management.

4. Armstrong & Hou Financial, Inc. Communicates Its Decisions

   Once Armstrong & Hou Financial, Inc.'s management has communicated its decisions, we will incorporate these decisions into the remaining design requirements.

5. Complete the Phase I Work Products

   a. Complete space requirements

      - Complete the space planning requirements for the data center to allow the architects and engineers to begin base building drawings.

Armstrong & Hou Financial, Inc.   9
Data Center Design

b. Electrical planning
   • Complete the electrical design development requirements
     within the data center. This includes:
       — Computer grounding requirements
       — Requirements for emergency power and
         uninterrupted power supply

c. Complete the remaining work products
   • Architectural requirements:
       — Raised floor height and loads
       — Exterior partition and wall approaches
   • Security system requirements:
       — Building interconnection approaches for alarms,
         detection and recordings
   • Fire protection requirements:
       — Halon/dry pipe approach requirements
   • High voltage AC and plumbing requirements:
       — Availability requirements
       — Routing of services to computer room

Phase II - Data Center Detailed Requirements

1. Complete the Phase II Work Products
   a. Complete space requirements
      • Complete the space planning requirements for the data
        center to allow the architects and engineers to begin bid
        package drawings. Completing the workstation
        requirements for this task would include:
          — Special lighting
          — Telephone and intercom
          — Console power requirements
          — Alarm panel

> — Security monitors
> — Partitions
> — Special doorways
- Complete the 1/4 scale hardware device layout
- Review locations and capacities for data center phone, power, and, if applicable, terminal cable distribution.

b. Electrical planning
- Complete the electrical requirements within the data center. This includes:
    > — Review cabling diagrams for the data center
    > — Computer grounding requirements
    > — Requirements for emergency power off controls

c. Complete the remaining work products
- Architectural requirements:
    > — Raised floor
    > — Hung ceiling
- Security system requirements:
    > — Alarms, detection, and recording
    > — Special access control
- Fire protection requirements:
    > — Interconnecting to other systems
- High Voltage AC and plumbing requirements:
    > — Pipe routing
    > — Flood protection

d. Vendor selection
- Identify vendors and pros and cons associated with specialty equipment to be used.

2. Review work products with Armstrong & Hou's management group.

3. Present work products to Armstrong & Hou's architect and engineer.

Armstrong & Hou Financial, Inc.   11
Data Center Design

IV. PROJECT RESULTS

Completion of the Data Center Design process in Phase I and II
described above will produce a set of deliverable drawings and requirements books. These results include the following.

Phase I

1. Block diagrams of computer room
   - Space layouts
   - Equipment distribution
2. Total loads for computer room
   - Kilowatts (KVA)
   - BTU levels
   - Weight
3. Requirements for closets
   - Location and capacities or circuit closets for
     — Power
     — Signal
     — Phone/data
4. Design development documents and sketches for
   - Electrical
     — Uninterrupted power supply
     — Emergency power
   - Security
   - Fire protection
   - High voltage AC
5. Weekly status meetings with AHF and its architect and engineer
   to review progress to date and refine schedules for completion of
   work products and support data gathering.

Armstrong & Hou Financial, Inc.   12
Data Center Design

Phase II

1. One-quarter inch layout and recommend considerations for computer room and adjacent area.
2. List of workstation components to be included for each workstation, such as:
   - Consoles
   - Special furniture and fixtures
   - Special lighting requirements
   - Telephones and/or intercoms
   - Alarm panels
   - Security monitors
   - Partitions
   - Special doorways
3. Raised floor requirements
   - Grid starting point
   - Ramps and stairs (if applicable)
   - Depth, composition, and cell and stringer system requirements
   - Slab sealing and cleaning requirements
4. Hung ceiling requirements
   - Material requirements
   - Composition and depth requirements for the cavity
   - Grid layout requirements
5. Electrical requirements
   - Load projections for:
     — Computers
     — High voltage AC
     — Lighting

Armstrong & Hou Financial, Inc.   13
Data Center Design

- Clean power and special protection requirements including:
    — Power distribution units and circuits
    — Motor generator sets
    — Emergency power off controls and circuits
    — Special grounding and fault isolation
    — Power protection alternatives:
        - Costs
        - Space, weight, and environmental characteristics
        - Historical reliability and availability
        - Statistics
- Detailed machine requirements:

    We will assemble the manufacturer specifications for the equipment models and identify receptacles, and provide tables for designing power distribution unit configurations.

6. Security systems plans including:
    - Requirements for detection, alarms and recording of environmental system failures and out of tolerance conditions (e.g., air conditioning unit failures, water leaks, etc.)
    - Requirements for special data center access control.

7. Fire protection systems including:
    - Cost/benefit trade-offs for backup fire protection methods (e.g., Halon and dry-pipe systems) to other security systems.

8. High voltage AC system requirements:
    - General high voltage AC requirements including:
        — Projected capacities for computer room air conditioning
        — Levels of redundancy in capacity, external dry-coolers, and pumps
        — Piping routing requirements
        — Special requirements for air handler installation (e.g., floor stands, etc.).

Armstrong & Hou Financial, Inc.   14
Data Center Design

9. Specialty plumbing including:
    • Layouts under raised floors
    • Requirements for floor drains
10. Vendor selections
    • Chart of specialized equipment vendors.

Armstrong & Hou Financial, Inc.   15
Data Center Design

V. TIME AND COST ESTIMATES

The following time and cost estimates are based on the RFP requirements and our experience with similar projects.

Time

The proposed team will complete the project on a timely basis, providing Armstrong & Hou Financial, Inc. with Design Development Requirements by October 15 and with the Data Center Detailed
Requirements within five weeks after receiving instructions from
Armstrong & Hou Financial, Inc. to proceed with the work.

Costs

We estimate the fees for this project will be as follows.

Phase I - Data Center Design Development
Requirements not to exceed $33,000

Phase II - Data Center Design Detailed
Requirements not to exceed $29,000

Phase III - Design Monitoring $10,000 to $15,000

Estimated costs for Phase I and II include travel expenses for one
person for each week of the project. Should Armstrong and Hou Financial, Inc. require additional travel for our staff, these expenses will be
in addition to the "not to exceed" amounts for Phases I and II.

We will estimate Phase III fees based on the requirements of
Armstrong and Hou Financial, Inc. at the conclusion of Phase II. In our
experience with similar relocation projects, Phase III costs are generally
within $10,000 to $15,000.

Armstrong & Hou Financial, Inc. will be invoiced for the consultant
fees plus actual out-of-pocket reimbursable expenses associated with
travel, computer usage, communications services, package delivery,
and report production twice per month. Within three months following
the conclusion of contracted services and the submission of a final
billing for these services, a project audit will be performed by Western
Consulting Associates. Any expenses not previously billed will be
invoiced to Armstrong & Hou Financial, Inc. at that time.

Armstrong & Hou Financial, Inc.   16
Data Center Design

VI. ORGANIZATION AND STAFFING

A key element in our approach to this project is the assignment of senior personnel who have significant data center design, planning, operations, and management experience. We have selected a project team that not only possesses a seasoned, realistic perspective but also can provide practical suggestions for improvement in such areas as workstation layouts, data center construction, and testing. The project team will consist of the following personnel:

Engagement Director	Dr. Ashok Nalamwar, Partner
Facility Requirements	Thomas S. Mitchell, Associate
Hardware and Network	Allen B. Donleavy, Managing Partner
Configuration Planning	A. Carla Wilson, Senior Consultant

We will report directly to Mr. Norman Winters, President. Due to the importance of this project for both organizations, Dr. Ashok Nalamwar, a Partner of our firm, has been assigned overall responsibility for this engagement.

We are anticipating that Armstrong & Hou Financial, Inc. personnel, architects, and engineers will be available to work with us. Such coordinated teamwork will greatly assist our data-gathering efforts during the early weeks of the project.

Armstrong & Hou Financial, Inc.   17
Data Center Design

VII. OUR EXPERIENCE AND QUALIFICATIONS

We believe that Western Consulting Associates is well qualified for this assignment. We have managed numerous data center design, construction, and relocation projects for organizations similar to Armstrong & Hou Financial, Inc. These firms include:

- Arthur D. Young and Company
- C. J. Lawrence, Morgan Grenfell, Inc.
- Crown Consolidated Industries
- Dean Witter Reynolds, Inc.
- Dollar Dry Dock
- G. D. Searle
- Glaxo, Inc.
- Memorial Sloan-Kettering Cancer Center
- Ogilvy and Mather
- Shearson Lehman Hutton
- Thomas and Betts
- Thomas McKinnon Securities, Inc.
- Ceco Corporation

The appendix to this proposal describes some of our most representative client assignments.

In addition, Western Consulting Associates project team members all have strong backgrounds in data processing operations and technical support management. Our senior staff has an average of 20 years experience in all areas of data center design, operations, systems, applications, technical support, and administration. Appendix B contains the resumes of project team members.

Armstrong & Hou Financial, Inc.   18
Data Center Design

APPENDIX

Armstrong & Hou Financial, Inc.   19
Data Center Design

REPRESENTATIVE CLIENT ASSIGNMENTS

During the past three years, we have conducted fourteen data center design assignments. The services provided ranged from assisting our clients and their architectural engineers in formulating the designs, through preparation of all construction documents and on-site supervision of construction and facility testing.

Arthur Young & Company

Developed the data center layout and prepared architectural and engineering plans for 8,500 square feet of data center space and the 40,000 square feet of adjacent office space to support their National Headquarters MIS, accounting offices and training center.

Memorial Sloan-Kettering Cancer Center

- Site Selection—responsible for the evaluation of several potential data center site locations. The study addressed availability of transportation services, communications, electrical power quality, availability of personnel, safety, and personnel services.

- Designs—we were asked by the hospital's facility management group to prepare the data center facility design requirements for a 17,000-square-foot facility and relocation plan consisting of over 800 specific tasks. The plan addressed the establishment of the new 308X-based facility located off-campus, reconfiguration of the present facility to support a reduced workload, and the establishment of satellite data centers for remote processing.

- Architectural and engineering—prepared the architectural and engineering drawings for construction activities, and monitored facility testing for uninterrupted power supply, Halon, high voltage AC, and access systems.

Shearson Lehman Hutton

Armstrong & Hou Financial, Inc.   20
Data Center Design

The client was in its third year of planning for a 1 million-square-foot data center, designed initially to support a configuration consisting of three 3090–400s, 3090–200, and a 3084. The network was comprised of 26 TI lines and 4800 twisted copper pairs. Our assignments included:

- Preparing construction bid specifications and a disciplined procedure for the installation and testing of the network control facility
- Assisting the client's staff in translating telecommunications design concepts into specific drawings and equipment specifications.

    Our role up to the production cutover included:

- Monitoring and revising the plan to address external factors (such as strikes and vendor slippages)
- Reviewing key project deliverables
- Assisting in coordinating user testing and final cutover.

    A second project for Shearson Lehman was to relocate its Commercial Paper operations from a remote site into the above centralized MIS facility. The configuration consisted of a dual Burrough's A9 complex with an international network consisting of 15 lines terminating at nine locations. Our assignment included:

- Designing 1,500-square-foot data center layout for the hardware and support functions
- Evaluating growth and associated workload and recommending hardware configuration.

Thomas McKinnon Securities, Inc.

Armstrong & Hou Financial, Inc.   21
Data Center Design

Thomas McKinnon Securities and its outside architects and engineers asked us to provide detailed requirements for its 22,000-square-foot data center designed for two 3090–400s and a 3081. The timeframe was extremely tight and required the coordination of our deliverables with the client and the architectural and engineering firms. In this way our work products were used directly by these firms to begin their designs, construction drawings, and equipment orders.

The work products included projections of hardware configurations over a 10-year period, research on cost trade-offs of alternative fire protection and electrical protection systems, detailed requirements for electrical, mechanical, plumbing, security, fire suppression, monitoring, and cabling, along with data used to select equipment vendors.

Once the initial bid package was prepared by the architectural and engineering firm, we conducted a detailed review for conformance to the original requirements.

Armstrong & Hou Financial, Inc.   22
Data Center Design

PROJECT STAFF RESUMES

Note: In your proposal, your project staff resumes will appear here. Please see this book's Appendix C: Sample Resume Boilerplates, following this sample proposal, for a complete selection of staff resumes.

APPENDIX
C

SAMPLE RESUME BOILERPLATES

≡Sample
Resume
Boilerplates

The following resumes are examples of boilerplate files that are included with a proposal (in the samples, all names are fictitious). The resumes can be tailored to emphasize staff experience in different areas as required by the proposal. Resumes on file are easy to update and can be reformatted for any type of document. (Appendix B contains the sample proposal for these resumes; Appendix A contains the Executive Summary for the proposal.)

When assembling resumes for your proposal, place them according to rank, usually as follows:

President/Partner

Vice President

Associate

Managing Partner/Director

Staff specialist (e.g., technical expert, physician, outside contractor)

Consultants

Support staff (if required)

Resumes can vary in length from one page to several pages, depending on the project and what the client needs to know about your proposed project staff. You want to show the client that your staff has the required credentials, experience, and ingenuity to complete the work to the client's satisfaction. Resume formats can vary, as well, but should always be clear and concise.

Armstrong & Hou Financial, Inc.   23
Data Center Design   Dr. Ashok Nalamwar

DR. ASHOK NALAMWAR

Dr. Nalamwar is a Partner of Western Consulting Associates. He received his B.S., M.S., and Ph.D. degrees from Stanford University. Dr. Nalamwar has twenty-four years of data processing experience in the banking, brokerage, insurance, medical, pharmaceutical, and manufacturing industries.

Dr. Nalamwar's main experiences have been in IBM Mainframe technical support, hardware and facilities planning, management and technical consulting, computer operations, applications development, distributed processing systems support, and micro systems support. He also has experience in relocating WANG, DEC, UNISYS, HP, IBM Sys 36/38, and Prime Systems.

MAJOR PROFESSIONAL ACCOMPLISHMENTS

As a management consultant, Dr. Nalamwar has participated in the planning and execution of four recent computer center relocations.

- *Major International Financial Services Firm*

  Consolidated data processing facilities from four sites into a single newly constructed facility in London, England. The relocation involved an upgrade from multiple dual 4381s to 3090s and the phased cutover of DEC 11/70 Systems and an IBM S/38. The data center supported on-line systems for New York, European, and Asian operations. Dr. Nalamwar's responsibilities included:

  — Development of project planning charts for each phase of the relocation

  — Development of all on-line, batch, and network testing and verification strategies

  — Project management including review of deliverables, task accounts and schedules, and management reporting on progress, and

Armstrong & Hou Financial, Inc.   24
Data Center Design   Dr. Ashok Nalamwar

— Implementation of a project management system for contract and scheduling of all tasks.

• *Major Pharmaceutical Firm*

Relocated the client's computer center and its operations, technical, and network support staffs to a newly renovated site within Chicago. The facility supported two 3081 processors with online users from coast to coast and throughout the country. Extremely tight controls were required as the cutover was conducted on a regular two-day weekend and involved moving many critical devices. Dr. Nalamwar's responsibilities were:

— Expansion of existing task list from approximately 90 to 300 tasks

— Implementation of project management systems for project scheduling control

— Assisted all project team members in defining deliverable requirements and formats

— Coordination of hardware vendor meetings

— Review of all task deliverables, project management system updating and analysis, and project status reporting

• *Major Manufacturing Firm*

The firm's entire computer center, support, and development staffs were relocated within Chicago to a newly constructed building and computer facility. A prerequisite to relocating was the need to consolidate from multi IBM mainframes to a single mainframe. Dr. Nalamwar's responsibilities were:

— Interviewing users and evaluating requirements for a nondisruptive move

— Development of processor replacement and relocation strategies and management support during their decision-making process

— Development of detailed task descriptions and planning charts for the processor swap and data center relocation

Armstrong & Hou Financial, Inc.   25
Data Center Design   Dr. Ashok Nalamwar

— Assisting the client in the implementation and initial
   execution of a project management system

• *Major Medical Center*

Assisted in decentralizing the medical center's computer data
processing center. The existing mainframes now run at the New
York site, and a 3081 system has been installed in a new facility
in New Jersey. Developed plans to upgrade later to a 3084 and
3090 configuration. All online applications were relocated to the
new computer center. Dr. Nalamwar's major responsibilities
were:

— Project manager for the relocation assignment tasks,
   deliverable dates, reviews, plan administration, and status
   reporting

— Design of computer room hardware layout, work station
   layouts, and office and storage layouts

— Implementation of the relocation project management system

— Development of a detailed hour-by-hour migration plan

— Creation of an application migration strategy and test plan

— Establishment of revised operational procedures for the
   coordination of both data centers.

PRIOR EXPERIENCE IN DATA PROCESSING

Prior to joining Western Consulting Associates, Dr. Nalamwar had a
distinguished career in data processing. Among his more outstanding
technical accomplishments are the following:

Major Commercial Bank

• Developed a Quality Assurance and Control function for a
  centralized operation of 18 DEC 11/70 and VAX systems that
  was being expanded to 28 systems. Developed and implemented

standards and procedures that addressed operating procedures, user applications, and operations interfacing, security, backups and restorers, and management controls.

- As an operating systems software project manager, responsible for the development and maintenance of all in-house system software and common subroutines, the analysis and implementation of vendor program products, and the creation of standards and procedures related to their use.

- As manager of Facilities and Hardware Planning, was responsible for:

  — Acquisition of all hardware for both the data center and all user areas. Major upgrades were the addition of a 3081 system, 3330 to 3350 DASD replacement, and 3211 to 3800 migration period.

  — Vendor and trade support of all environmental systems including UPS system with diesels, electrical distribution, air conditioning systems, and fire protection systems.

- As project leader for an on-line trust system supporting 200 terminals, dealt with all maintenance for the CICS/IMS data base oriented portion of the system, performance tuning and enhancements to support end-user processing using tools such as FOCUS and programmer productivity tools such as MANTIS.

- Performed capacity study of the Employee Benefit Trust accounting and reporting system to determine the impacts and requirements associated with the integration of the Personal Trust system. The study addressed the processor, auxiliary storage, network, response time, and batch throughput capacity issues.

National Facility Management Company

- Major Insurance Company: Responsible for the development of a plan to move all the OS software from New York City to a new Data Processing Center in Roanoke, Virginia. The task

Armstrong & Hou Financial, Inc.   27
Data Center Design   Dr. Ashok Nalamwar

included the testing and verification of all hardware, software, and data following the move. This plan was executed starting with the close of business on a Friday and was ready the following Monday morning in the new facility.

- Major Brokerage Firms: The clients commissioned a joint study to develop and implement a mainframe-to-mainframe inquiry and retrieval facility. This task was part of a data processing start-up project at both clients' sites.

- Major Consumer Products Manufacturer: Responsible for the start-up of a facility to support new systems development and production processing. This task involved the implementation of all support facilities, training of operations and applications staff, and development of standards and procedures for operating, controlling, and securing the operation. The facility was up and running in two weeks, and two months later, the first application was in production.

Armstrong & Hou Financial, Inc.   28
Data Center Design   Thomas S. Mitchell

THOMAS S. MITCHELL

Mr. Mitchell is an Associate of Western Consulting Associates. He holds a B.S. degree from Carnegie Mellon University of Pittsburgh, and an M.S. degree from the University of Illinois. He has seventeen years experience in data processing in the manufacturing, financial services, and telecommunications industries. His areas of expertise include management consulting, data processing operations, hardware planning, and applications development.

MAJOR PROFESSIONAL ACCOMPLISHMENTS

Mr. Mitchell's major consulting achievements include the following:

- Developed Western Consulting Associates' approach to computer center relocation, consolidation, and design. In the past five years, he developed relocation plans for:
  — Three major brokerage firms
  — Two major banks
  — A "Big-six" accounting firm
  — Several manufacturers

- *Major Brokerage Firm*

  Prepared the consolidation plan for a major brokerage firm which relocated its data center from New York to Dallas, established a large satellite network to a corporate network, and absorbed the data processing for a large credit card and banking subsidiary.

- *Major Medical Center*

  Prepared the data center facility design and relocation plan for a large medical center. The plan addressed establishing the new 3081 based facility located off-campus, reconfiguration of the present on-campus facility to support a reduced workload, and establishing satellite centers for remote processing.

Armstrong & Hou Financial, Inc.   29
Data Center Design   Thomas S. Mitchell

- *Major Commercial Bank*

  Developed an integrated technical, operational, and facilities plan for the client's multiple data centers to address cost reduction, security, growth, disaster recovery, and business risks associated with relocation and consolidation. The study led to a multimillion-dollar reduction in operating costs, improved security, additional capacity to meet growth, and an improved image for marketing the bank's services.

- *Major Domestic Conglomerate*

  Mr. Mitchell has been retained on an ongoing assignment to assist this $1.2 billion diversified organization in its annual MIS strategic planning process. Key directions he is implementing with the staff are:

  — Improved payback associated to development projects, and software and hardware upgrades

  — Improved responsiveness of MIS to changing business needs

  — Improved information and processing security

- *Cellular Telephone Services Supplier*

  Reviewed the implementation and production support of the primary business stem for this Fortune 10 company. The study led to applications systems revisions, a reorganization of the applications maintenance and operations support functions, a relocation of the application to a more stable operating environment, and modifications to user operating procedures. Customer service levels were improved and key clients were served more efficiently.

- *Large Investment Bank*

  Performed a comprehensive security review of the trading, research, office automation and back office systems to identify physical, data, application, software, and operational exposures. The findings showed major risks of disclosure, operational disruptions, and tampering. A practical approach to address these exposures was developed and implemented.

Armstrong & Hou Financial, Inc.   30
Data Center Design   Thomas S. Mitchell

- *Major Pharmaceutical Firm*

  Developed the contingency plan strategy and implementation
  plan for this large scale IBM, HP, DEC, and Prime based firm.
  This involved selection of methods to switch its on-campus IBM
  Token Ring, Ethernet, and remote network to a backup site;
  preparation of detailed procedures that have to be in place prior
  to execution of a disaster recovery; and development of
  procedures to keep the Plan current. The company has recently
  conducted their first test and is working towards the plan
  completion.

PRIOR EXPERIENCE IN DATA PROCESSING

Before joining Western Consulting Associates, Mr. Mitchell acquired
the following data processing operations experience:

First National Bank

- As manager of hardware and capacity planning, he was
  responsible for capacity and hardware planning studies on
  methods to increase capacity in a growth environment hardware;
  implementation storage management operational performance
  and capacity reporting; and implementation of a chargeback
  system for an MVS environment with IMS, CICS,
  INTERCOMM, and JES3 software systems.

Inland Steel

- As a project leader of systems software, he was responsible for
  implementation and support of an automated data processing
  production control system within multiple data centers. Prior to
  this position he was an operations analyst during the conversion
  of all corporate systems to IBM 360 processors in an ASP

Armstrong & Hou Financial, Inc.   31
Data Center Design   Thomas S. Mitchell

environment. Responsibilities included diagnosis and resolution of hardware, applications, operational, and systems software problems. He also held positions at U.S. Steel as an applications programmer/analyst supporting on-line order entry and sales analysis systems.

Armstrong & Hou Financial, Inc.   32
Data Center Design   Allen B. Donleavy

ALLEN B. DONLEAVY

Mr. Donleavy is a Managing Partner with the Information Services Group of Western Consulting Associates. He received his B.S. degree from Ohio University and his M.S. and M.B.A. degrees from Michigan State University. He has seventeen years experience in data processing.

Mr. Donleavy's technical experience has been in large scale mainframe online and network support, telecommunications, hardware, facilities planning, and applications development. His management work has focused on overseeing distributed processing operations, money transfer wire rooms, check processing, and large scale data centers.

MAJOR PROFESSIONAL ACCOMPLISHMENTS

Mr. Donleavy's most recent consulting achievements for data processing projects include:

- *Major Brokerage Firm:*

  Responsible for the phaseover installation and testing for one of the largest brokerage data centers in New York. As the senior consultant for this effort, Mr. Donleavy:

  — Developed short and long-term communications equipment requirements and the firm's associated cabling, space, electrical, and mechanical loads (both primary and backup)

  — Developed architectural and engineering requirements including:

    • Hardware configuration and layouts for network equipment

    • Workstation components within network control facilities

    • Cabling specifications for office areas, interconnections between communications equipment, voice distribution rooms, and cabling distribution rooms for fiber and copper circuits

Armstrong & Hou Financial, Inc.   33
Data Center Design   Allen B. Donleavy

- Fiber/copper facilities within the building riser systems
- Electrical requirements for power protection, lighting, grounding
- Vendor selection considerations

— Developed implementation plans to accomplish the network phaseover and coordinated external/in-house network installation, site construction/testing activities, and computer equipment installation/testing

— Site supervision of network construction activities

- *Major Brokerage Firm, London, England*

Consolidated all business functions, technical support, and computer and telecommunication services of this international firm from five locations to a single new facility. This included multiple data centers (IBM, DEC, and Wang) and a global telecommunications network to support the new facility and all European and Far East branches. Mr. Donleavy's specific responsibilities included:

— Developed detailed plans for installation and testing of the telecommunications hardware for voice/data systems.

— Coordinated vendor activities among multiple vendors and suppliers.

— Coordinated testing among United States, European, and Far East branches.

- *Major Pharmaceutical Firm*

Developed detailed plan to relocate into a 12,000-square-foot data center. The data processing environment consisted of IBM, HP, Prime, and DEC mainframes. Also developed plans to design, install and implement interconnections among the various mainframes using Ethernet, IBM Token Ring, and SNA Gateway. Reviewed a backbone network consisting of two fiber optics rings connecting the data center to a primary and backup central office.

Armstrong & Hou Financial, Inc.   34
Data Center Design   Allen B. Donleavy

- *Major Accounting Firm*

  Designed the new data center for a large professional accounting
  firm. This assignment resulted in layouts for network control
  center for voice and data, the hardware components (CPUs, disk
  drives, tape drives), console area, printer pool, and tape library,
  and development of requirements for hardware vendors,
  engineers, and architects.

- *Major Medical Center*

  Responsible for the evaluation of several potential data center
  site locations. This assignment included evaluating
  communications, transportation facilities, electrical power
  quality, availability of personnel, safety, and personnel services
  (e.g., restaurants, shopping, banking parking).

PRIOR EXPERIENCE IN DATA PROCESSING

Before joining the Data Processing Group of Western Consulting Associates, Mr. Donleavy served as Senior Data Manager at a major
commercial bank. His accomplishments included the following:

- Managed a large scale data center operations department
  comprised of three 308X scale processors, supporting over 700
  online users in an MVS/JES3, IMS, CICS environment.
  Functional areas of responsibility were:
  — Network scheduling and control center
  — Consoles
  — Printer pool
  — Tape pool/tape library
  — COM lab
  — Operation technicians
  — Remote job entry sites
  — Library maintenance and control

Armstrong & Hou Financial, Inc.   35
Data Center Design   Allen B. Donleavy

- Planned and controlled the budget, hardware and personnel expenses for the Data Center. Major accomplishments were:
  — Planned and installed all online user's communication hardware
  — Planned and installed remote job entry sites
  — Reduced staff by means of changes in work flow, purchase of labor saving products, and conversion of tab equipment processing to the mainframe
  — Planned and coordinated major processor upgrades from 370 to 308X technology and installation of high density DASD devices.
- As a member of the online technical support group, during the relocation of the bank's data center he was responsible for:
  — Design of the network control center
  — Development of plans for installation and testing of all data communications equipment
  — Maintenance of the online monitor INTERCOMM
  — Support of online application support programmers
  — Development of in-house code to perform restart/recovery for online applications
  — Support of the migration of applications from INTERCOMM to CICS
- As a manager of distributed processing, he was responsible for the data center operation of staff and hardware spread across the following equipment:
  — Digital - PDP 11/70 and PDP 11/45
  — Burroughs - B2700
  — IBM - S370 158
  — Mohawk Data System - 2400

Armstrong & Hou Financial, Inc.   36
Data Center Design   A. Carla Wilson

A. CARLA WILSON

Ms. Wilson is a Senior Consultant with the Information Services Group of Western Consulting Associates. As a consultant, Ms. Wilson specializes in management information systems. She received a B.A. degree from the Pennsylvania State University and a M.B.A. degree from the University of Pittsburgh. Ms. Wilson has fifteen years of business and data processing experience. Her primary areas of expertise are in the management of information systems, warehousing and distribution, and cost accounting and statistical analysis.

MAJOR PROFESSIONAL ACCOMPLISHMENTS

As a consultant, Ms. Wilson recently completed the following projects:

- Computer center design and relocation planning for several companies including:
  - Three major brokerage firms
  - Major financial services firm
  - Two major pharmaceutical firms
  - Three medium-sized manufacturing firms
  - Major bank
  - Major accounting firm
  - Two large medical centers
- Overall reviews of data processing activities and centralization/decentralization studies for several organizations including the following:
  - A European multinational electronics and appliance manufacturer
  - A multibillion-dollar diverse conglomerate
  - A leading commodities trading company

Armstrong & Hou Financial, Inc.   37
Data Center Design   A. Carla Wilson

    — One of the "Seven Sisters" oil companies

    — A major southern electric utility

    — A large public housing authority

- Computer capacity planning/hardware acquisition engagements for several organizations including the following:

    — A leading investment trading corporation

    — A major conglomerate

    — A major southwestern utility company

    — A multinational electronics and appliance manufacturer

    — A major middle-Atlantic states bank

    — Two large medical centers

PRIOR DATA PROCESSING EXPERIENCE

Prior to her consulting career, Ms. Wilson successfully planned and executed three computer center relocations as follows:

United States Steel Corporation

- The Western Regional Data Center was moved to and merged into the Central Regional Data Center. In the process all hardware in the Central RDC was replaced, as was all operating system software. Ms. Wilson's specific responsibilities were technical planning, configuration definition, and technical trouble shooting for the first year of operation of the new site.

Bankers Trust Company

- Ms. Wilson had primary responsibility for relocating the bank's main computer center from Wall Street to a new operations building at 1 Bankers Trust Plaza. Her responsibilities included development of the configurations of hardware (migration from

Armstrong & Hou Financial, Inc.   38
Data Center Design   A. Carla Wilson

IBM 165 to IBM 168 technology), overall logistical planning for and execution of the physical move, and definition of and installation of teleprocessing equipment. She achieved the following:

— Cutover was complete within 24 hours with no disruption to the user community

— Move was completed on schedule and under budget

— Computer center was fully backed up

— Configurations developed included three large-scale mainframes, 54 disk units, 30,000-reel magnetic tape library, and 500-line teleprocessing network.

Scholastic, Inc.

• Ms. Wilson had overall responsibility for information systems as well as warehousing and distribution responsibilities when she relocated Scholastic's Information Center for northern New Jersey to the Meadowlands. This relocation involved four medium-scale mainframes and 250 clerical and professional personnel.

• The move was completed over a three-day holiday with no disruption to business and was accomplished on time and under budget.

≡INDEX

≡About the Authors

ROBERT J. HAMPER was with the Bell System for over 11 years and often evaluated proposals from outside consultants and specialized firms. At Bell, he held a variety of positions in such areas as market analysis, economic evaluation, market management, strategic planning, and financial management. At Bell, he designed and implemented practical applications of portfolio theory and optimization modeling of resource allocation to the strategic market/planning process.

Mr. Hamper also has worked at AT&T and with Bell Laboratories on modeling techniques for practical use in financial and strategic market planning. He holds B.S.B.A. and M.B.A. degrees from Illinois State University and is an adjunct professor in the Graduate School of Business at Rosary College. Mr. Hamper is president of his own consulting firm, which specializes in strategic planning.

L. SUE BAUGH was senior editor for six years at Booz, Allen & Hamilton, Inc., one of the largest management consultant firms in the world. As part of the Report Production department, Ms. Baugh helped to develop, write, and produce numerous proposals responding to bids from industry, government, and nonprofit associations.

Ms. Baugh is currently an independent business writer and has contributed to and edited numerous books on marketing, finance, and related business topics. She holds a B.A. degree from the University of Iowa and an M.A. degree from the University of North Carolina.